HARPER CHASE

Nefarious Crimes: Unsolved Murders Vol. 2

First edition

Contents

Introduction

In the shadow-laden recesses of our collective history, there exist mysteries so profound, so impenetrable, that their echoes reverberate across the annals of time, defiant in their refusal to be silenced. These enigmatic tales, the unsolved murders that have seized the public's imagination, stumped the most brilliant minds, and stood stubbornly just beyond the veil of comprehension, form the core of this book. Herein lies a deep dive into these enigmatic tales—a sojourn through the darkest alleys of human actions and the serpentine paths of investigation that have, thus far, led us down a rabbit hole of more questions than answers.

What is it about the unresolved that captivates us so? Why do these chilling, often brutal, acts of violence, left without closure, continue to haunt the recesses of our minds? Is it an inherent human craving for resolution, or perhaps the tantalizing allure of the unknown? As you delve into the pages of this book, you will be transported into the realm of the unsolved—a world where every clue, every suspect, and every theory could be the elusive key to unraveling a mystery that has, until now, lurked in the shadows.

As we navigate these tales, we recount not just the grisly details and the relentless pursuit for answers but also delve deep into the psychological, social, and cultural reverberations of these crimes. Unsolved murders are not mere isolated incidents; they are mirrors reflecting the societies in which they occur, echoing our deepest fears, our obsessions, and the collective psyche of humanity. They challenge our beliefs in justice and the perceived infallibility of law enforcement, leaving us in a lingering state of disquiet.

Immersing yourself in these narratives, you will grapple with theories and suspects, ranging from the plausible to the wildly speculative. You will witness the evolution of criminal investigation techniques and the profound impact of media on shaping public perception. But, most poignantly, you will confront the human cost of these crimes—the victims, their families, and the communities irrevocably scarred by these acts of violence.

As the book progresses, we delve into the very nature of these unsolved cases. What does it mean for a murder to remain unsolved in an era where technology and forensic science have scaled unprecedented heights? How do these cold cases continue to mold our understanding of justice and closure? And, in a haunting reflection, what are the chances that the veils shrouding these mysteries will ever be lifted?

Closing this book, the echoes of these unsolved murders will persist, a testament to the enduring power of the unknown and the unresolved. These stories transcend mere tales of death and mystery; they are profound windows into the human condition, deep explorations into the darkest corners of our nature, and stark reminders of the fragile thread that separates order from chaos. Welcome to a journey into the heart of the unresolved, where every chapter challenges you to look beyond the surface, to question the accepted narrative, and to contemplate the complex tapestry of human existence that is both terrifyingly dark and infinitely fascinating.

Murder of Paul Jones

On the serene evening of Wednesday, May 4, 1983, Melody Ann Jones, a 19-year-old with a cheerful spirit, enjoyed a tranquil fishing trip at Shawnee Twin Lakes in Oklahoma. Accompanying her were her doting parents and her siblings, with whom she shared an exceptionally close bond. These fishing excursions had become a beloved ritual for the tight-knit family, offering them moments of joy and togetherness.

As the day waned, Melody's younger brother, Randall Garton, a thoughtful and caring sibling, offered to drive her back to the cozy home she shared with her husband, Paul Richard Jones, a young man of 20 years, located on the picturesque Benson Park Road in Earlsboro. They reached Melody's abode around 10:30 p.m., under a sky sprinkled with stars.

Upon their arrival, Randall noticed the warm glow of the house's lights spilling onto the lawn as Melody stepped into her home. Inside, the lights cast a welcoming ambiance, and a man's silhouette was visible in the doorway. Randall, without a second thought, assumed the figure to be Paul, Melody's husband.

In a gesture of sisterly affection, Melody invited Randall to stay over for the night, an invitation he had accepted numerous times before. However, on this fateful night, Randall chose to return to his own home, unaware of the harrowing events that were about to unfold.

The following morning brought with it an unsettling silence. Melody, known for her punctuality and dedication, failed to show up for her shift at the local Dairy Queen in Seminole. This unusual absence alarmed one of her colleagues, prompting a concerned call to Melody's mother, Carol Garton. Carol, equally puzzled by her daughter's uncharacteristic no-show, felt a growing sense of unease.

Driven by worry, Carol hurried to the Jones' residence, a place once filled with laughter and love. What she discovered there was a scene of unimaginable horror. Inside the couple's bedroom lay Paul Jones, lifeless and brutally stabbed. The police later confirmed the tragic demise. Near the foot of the bed, a .12 gauge shotgun, typically stationed in a corner of the room, hinted at the chaos of the night.

Amidst the disarray, Melody was nowhere to be found. Her glasses and purse, personal items she regularly used, were left behind. The contents of her purse were scattered across the floor, a silent testament to the night's turmoil.

Outside, Paul and Melody's car sat untouched in the driveway. A frantic search by Carol for her daughter yielded no results. With a heart heavy with dread, she reached out to the Pottawatomie Sheriff's Office, reporting the gruesome murder of her son-in-law and the mysterious disappearance of her beloved daughter, Melody.

As the mystery of Melody Ann Jones' disappearance and the death of her husband Paul deepened, the local police swiftly converged on their home, determined to uncover clues. On arrival, they meticulously combed through the house, seeking any signs that might explain the tragic events of that night. However, their investigation revealed no evidence of a robbery, forced entry, or even a domestic dispute. Everything in the couple's home appeared to be in its rightful place, leaving the family and authorities perplexed.

In the wake of the tragedy, Marge Jones, Paul's mother, was granted permission to enter the home. As she stepped into the house, a place now shadowed by sorrow, she became increasingly convinced that her son's murder had not occurred there. Marge recalled the distinct yellow and white shag carpet that adorned the house in 2015. Her observations were startling. The carpet, walls, and curtains were devoid of any bloodstains, a puzzling absence given the violent nature of Paul's death. Marge remembered a past incident vividly: when Paul had accidentally sliced his foot with an ax, blood had spurted everywhere, a stark contrast to the current bloodless scene. Her questions echoed in the silent rooms: why was there no blood spatter?

Travis Palmer, the Undersheriff of the Pottawatomie Sheriff's Office, reflected on the evidence. The photographs from the crime scene neither confirmed nor contradicted Marge's theory about the murder taking place elsewhere. He acknowledged that such a significant detail was unlikely to be overlooked by the Oklahoma State Bureau of Investigation (OSBI).

The police, determined to solve this enigmatic case, carried out extensive ground searches. They maintained detailed records, painstakingly document-ing each step of their investigation. Despite their efforts, the truth behind Melody's involvement, whether as a participant in the homicide or as a victim kidnapped afterward, remained elusive.

Palmer, in a conversation with "Dateline," expressed the complexity of the situation. The puzzle of what exactly transpired that night continued to baffle them. The authorities remained committed to unraveling the truth, holding onto hope that someday they would make sense of the tragic events that had unfolded in the quiet home.

In the wake of the tragic events on May 4th, Marge Jones, fueled by a desperate need for answers, embarked on a personal investigation. She approached the neighbors of Paul and Melody, hoping they might have witnessed something on that fateful night. Her inquiries revealed that some neighbors had indeed heard disturbing sounds: yelling, screaming, and the violent slamming of doors and car doors, accompanied by the screech of tires. These revelations hinted at a chaotic scene, yet, frustratingly, the neighbors were reluctant to share more. Fear seemed to grip them, making them hesitant to speak further with the authorities.

Marge also found herself reflecting on past conversations with Melody, especially those during their time working together as housekeepers at a Shawnee hotel. Melody, an avid soap opera fan, often had the shows playing in the background. Marge recalled a chilling remark made by Melody, where she casually mentioned her belief that she could get away with murder. This statement, initially dismissed by Marge as a bizarre fascination with her soap operas, now took on a more sinister tone. Melody had even spoken about the ease of obtaining a new social security card and driver's license on the street, further adding to the unsettling nature of their past conversations.

The pursuit of truth, however, came at a cost for Marge. She began receiving menacing phone calls, replete with threats, as she continued to probe into the case. The anonymous calls, particularly one that included a direct threat to her life, spoken in a male voice, forced her to retreat from her investigations, leaving her with a deep sense of unease and unanswered questions.

Meanwhile, the official investigation encountered its own set of challenges. The murder weapon, a critical piece of evidence, remained elusive. In June 1983, as the Jones family sifted through the belongings in Paul and Melody's home, they discovered a pair of scissors in a drawer. Connecting it to the nature of Paul's wounds, they promptly handed it over to the Oklahoma State Bureau of Investigation (OSBI). This potential lead seemed promising, as the OSBI arranged for the scissors to be compared to skin samples from Paul's body.

However, a baffling turn of events followed. According to an OSBI document dated April 16, 1985, the skin samples, crucial for comparison, mysteriously disappeared. The document detailed how the samples, retained during the autopsy, had been lost, an oversight that raised serious questions about the handling of evidence. The inexplicable delay of almost two years to transport the scissors for comparison and the subsequent misplacement of the samples added layers of complexity and frustration to an already convoluted case.

As the investigation continued, authorities unearthed a potentially significant lead. They discovered the existence of at least one life insurance policy on Paul, with the possibility of a second one. This revelation opened a new avenue in the quest to understand the motives behind the tragic events.

In 2015, Marge Jones, Paul's mother, shared a crucial piece of information. She revealed that one of the life insurance policies had become effective just under a month before her son's murder. This policy, dated April 22, 1983, bore Paul's signature but notably lacked any mention of Melody, both in terms of her name and signature. The terms of the policy stipulated that the surviving spouse would be the primary beneficiary, entitled to the payout. However, in the absence of a surviving spouse, the proceeds were to be directed into an estate.

Intriguingly, as of April 1985, two years after the policy took effect, there was no record of any claims having been made against it. This detail added a layer of complexity to the case, leaving investigators to ponder the significance of this policy in the broader context of the investigation.

Further deepening the mystery, court records hinted at the existence of more than one insurance policy. Paul's father, Jack Jones, had filed a petition to be appointed as the administrator of his son's estate, a request that was granted by Judge Glenn Dale Carter. Among the documents submitted by Jack was a receipt dated February 11, 1983. This receipt, categorized as an insurance payment to American General Life, totaled $960.78 and appeared to be for a different policy than the one Marge had referenced in her conversation with the _Red Dirt Report_.

Financial troubles also seemed to plague Paul and Melody. Records indicated that in February 1983, one of them had closed an overdrawn checking account and subsequently opened a new one at a different bank. A credit card statement dated May 9, 1983, further revealed an overdrawn account with a previous cash advance exceeding $400, painting a picture of financial instability.

Another angle explored in the investigation was the potential involvement of drug use, although this theory was met with strong opposition from the Jones family. Rumors circulated about the couple's possible marijuana use, but Marge firmly denied any such activities on her son's part. The medical examiner's report, while negating the presence of alcohol in Paul's system, did not explicitly mention testing for drugs, leaving this aspect of their life shrouded in uncertainty.

In the ongoing quest to unravel the mysteries, numerous witness reports emerged, adding intriguing yet elusive leads. Marge Jones, Paul's mother, firmly believed she had seen Melody driving along the road where the couple once lived. This sighting, if accurate, was a significant development, hinting at Melody's possible survival after the incident. Furthermore, a neighbor reported seeing Melody on the property, noting an unusual detail - a bus with Mexican license plates nearby.

Adding to these mysterious sightings, a report surfaced from Port Lavaca, Texas, a location with a personal connection to the family, as Marge mentioned they owned a cabin there. A woman in this area claimed she had given Melody a ride to Cutler, Texas, providing a potential clue to her whereabouts. Additionally, there was a reported sighting in Oklahoma City, further expanding the geographical scope of the investigation.

In a potentially related case, the disappearance of 18-year-old Patricia Ann Hamilton on April 9, 1983, added another layer of mystery. Patricia vanished while working a night shift at a Seminole convenience store, and her remains were tragically found eight years later in Konawa, OK. The circumstances of her disappearance and death, including a "no sale" transaction at 4:35 a.m. and $114 missing from the register, bore a haunting similarity to the Jones case. However, despite these parallels, no concrete evidence linked the two cases.

A new clue emerged in 2015 when someone discovered a ruby ring on the property of Paul and Melody Jones' former home. Melody was known to have worn a ruby ring before her disappearance, making this find potentially significant. Investigators conducted a thorough search of the property for more evidence, but unfortunately, their efforts yielded no further clues. The couple's former home, which might have held more answers, had been destroyed in a 2014 grass fire, erasing any lingering traces of the past.

In a novel approach to uncovering new information, the police announced in February 2019 their plan to distribute playing cards featuring details of Paul's murder and Melody's disappearance to prison inmates. This initiative aimed to jog the memories of inmates who might possess knowledge about the case. Additionally, the authorities had DNA samples from the family members on file with NamUs (National Missing and Unidentified Persons System), holding onto hope that these efforts might finally shed light on the enduring mystery of what happened to Melody Ann Jones and who was responsible for Paul's tragic death.

Silver Bridge Collapse

Point Pleasant, nestled along the serene banks of the Ohio River, presents an intriguing blend of history and folklore. Established in 1774 as a military fortification, this small town quickly became a historical landmark due to the pivotal Battle of Point Pleasant. This conflict, a significant chapter in Lord Dunmore's War, marked a decisive moment in the early American frontier.

The battle unfolded in an era when the region was largely uncharted by white settlers, leading to heightened tensions between Lord Dunmore, the British representative, and the local Native American tribes. The Native American forces, valiantly led by Chief Cornstalk, engaged in a fierce struggle for their lands against the encroaching settlers.

Chief Cornstalk, a figure of both respect and tragedy, emerged as a central character in this saga. Following the battle, in a disheartening turn of events, he was treacherously killed by Virginians during what was supposed to be a peaceful negotiation. His final resting place lies in the heart of Point Pleasant, adding a somber note to its historical landscape.

The legacy of Chief Cornstalk and the Battle of Point Pleasant has evolved into local lore, with some considering the subsequent misfortunes in the area as a result of "Chief Cornstalk's Curse." This legend, though unproven, adds a mystical dimension to the town's history, intertwining facts and myths. While there's no concrete evidence to suggest Chief Cornstalk harbored any resentment towards the settlers, his story remains a poignant reminder of the complex and often turbulent interactions between Native Americans and early American settlers.

The enigmatic tale of Point Pleasant, a quaint town with a rich historical tapestry and a tight-knit community, took a turn towards the extraordinary on November 2nd, 1966. It was a period when Point Pleasant, nestled by the Ohio River, was a familiar place where neighbors knew each other's names and stories.

The central figure in this peculiar chapter was Woodrow Derenberger, a resident of Mineral Wells, located about an hour northwest of Point Pleasant. Derenberger, a traveling salesman, was making his way home from a work trip across the Ohio River on that fateful evening. His journey along Interstate 77 would soon become the stuff of local legend.

Derenberger's own recounting of the events from that November evening paints a vivid picture. He describes an encounter at around 7:30 PM with an unorthodox vehicle, resembling a car but capable of hovering just above the ground. This vehicle, according to his account, overtook him and then abruptly stopped in front, forcing him to a halt.

Here, the story takes a leap into the incredible. Derenberger claimed that the occupant of this vehicle was a being named "Cold," possessing a human-like appearance but communicating telepathically. This aspect of the story, with its echoes of the era's fascination with UFOs and extraterrestrial encounters, stretches the bounds of credibility for many.

Yet, Derenberger stood by his extraordinary claim. He recounted a brief interaction with this entity, Cold, who maintained a constant grin — a feature that would later inspire the nickname "The Grinning Man." According to Derenberger, Cold's parting words were a promise of future communication.

What adds an intriguing layer to this story is the timing. Derenberger reported his encounter on the very night it happened, a detail captured in the interview being discussed. This incident marked the beginning of a series of strange occurrences in and around Point Pleasant, setting the stage for a period of heightened curiosity and speculation in the community.

The story of Woodrow Derenberger and his alleged encounter with an extraterrestrial being named "Cold" is one that invites skepticism and doubt. Over the years, many have dismissed his claims as mere fabrications. Yet, Derenberger's narrative, coming from a seemingly ordinary background, adds an intriguing layer to the saga.

Derenberger, at the time a 50-year-old sewing machine salesman, embodied the archetype of the American dream. Married and a father, he appeared to be just another everyday man you might encounter in mid-1960s West Virginia. There was nothing in his history to suggest a propensity for fantastical stories or attention-seeking behavior.

However, his extraordinary claims thrust him into the limelight, casting a shadow over his reputation and mental stability. In the close-knit communities of the American Northeast, such stories were sensational, and Derenberger found himself under intense public scrutiny. Curiosity seekers and skeptics alike camped outside his home, some hidden, others overt, all searching for evidence of the alleged UFOs. Meanwhile, his personal life began to unravel under the weight of widespread disbelief and ridicule.

Interestingly, others in the vicinity reported seeing unusual phenomena on the night of November 2nd. While none corroborated meeting the telepathic Cold, several witnesses described seeing unexplainable, fast-moving lights in the sky, exhibiting behavior unlike any known aircraft of the time.

Derenberger maintained that his communication with Cold continued, claiming these interactions were telepathic, spanning across distances. He purported to learn more about Cold and his supposed home planet, Lanulos.

His experiences led him to author "Visitors From Lanulos," a memoir published in 1971, but this only served to further fuel public skepticism. Derenberger's life took a downward spiral; he lost his job, his marriage collapsed, and he faced the heartbreak of losing custody of his children.

Despite the severe personal and social costs, Derenberger never retracted his statements. He remained steadfast in his belief that his encounters with the Grinning Man, a being he claimed seldom brought good tidings, were genuine.

In the wake of Woodrow Derenberger's unusual claims, the local region began buzzing with corroborating reports of strange sightings, particularly of mysterious lights in the sky. The intrigue intensified on November 12th when an event occurred that would forever change the local folklore.

In Clendenin, a town located about an hour southeast of Point Pleasant, a group of five gravediggers made a startling claim. They reported seeing a bizarre, large, winged entity emerging from a clump of trees. This being, described more like a winged man than any recognizable bird, swooped over the men, its proximity evoking fear and awe.

This encounter marked the first reported sighting of what would soon be known as the Mothman, a name that would become synonymous with the mysteries of the area.

A few days later, on November 15th, another peculiar incident occurred, this time involving Newell Partridge in Salem, West Virginia, situated two hours northeast of Point Pleasant. Partridge was at home around 10:30 PM when he was startled by a sudden, loud, whining noise from outside, coinciding with his television displaying static and strange patterns. The noise, which he likened to a generator starting up, caught the attention of his German Shepherd, Bandit.

Following Bandit's lead, Partridge, armed only with a flashlight, ventured towards his barn, about 500 feet from the house. There, in the darkness, his flashlight beam met with a pair of large, glowing red eyes. Overwhelmed by fear, Partridge retreated to his house to arm himself, but found himself too petrified to confront the unknown entity again.

Tragically, according to local legend, Partridge never saw Bandit again after that night.

The Mothman sightings didn't end there. Later that same night, this enigmatic creature was reportedly seen again in Point Pleasant, over a hundred miles from Partridge's encounter.

In the era of World War II, the outskirts of Point Pleasant witnessed the establishment of the West Virginia Ordnance Works. This facility was crucial for the war effort, focusing on the production and storage of explosives. The munitions were kept in steel structures, colloquially known as "igloos," by the locals. Long after the war's end, these bunkers, enveloped by nature's embrace, remained largely undisturbed, giving rise to what locals would call "the TNT area."

By the evening of November 15th, this TNT area, a relic of wartime activities now reclaimed by the wilderness, had gained a different reputation, evolving into a sort of local hangout, particularly among the youth. It was here that two young couples, Rodger and Linda Scarberry, and Steve and Mary Mallette, decided to spend their evening. The TNT area, secluded and nestled in the wooded landscape, had become a popular spot akin to a lover's lane.

However, their visit coincided with the unsettling events surrounding the Mothman, just hours after Newell Partridge's alleged encounter. As they drove near a power plant within the TNT area, the couples reported sighting a large, humanoid figure with expansive bat-like wings and notably intense red eyes. Their descriptions were consistent, emphasizing the creature's extraordinary height and its ominous presence.

Terrified by this encounter, the couples fled in their car, racing towards Point Pleasant. Their drive home turned into a harrowing experience, with the creature purportedly keeping pace with them at speeds reaching 100 miles per hour. According to their accounts, the Mothman pursued them, its red eyes a constant, unnerving presence.

Upon nearing Point Pleasant, the creature seemingly retreated. The couples, still shaken, sought help at the local courthouse where they met Deputy Sheriff Millard Halstead. In a small town like Point Pleasant, where faces are familiar and stories are shared, Halstead knew these young people and recognized the gravity of their distress. He listened intently to their story, lending credence to their extraordinary encounter.

In response to the unsettling accounts from the Scarberrys and Mallettes, the authorities of Point Pleasant held a press conference to address the community's growing concerns. The aim was to reassure the public and provide a rational explanation for the bizarre sightings. The consensus was that the hysteria surrounding these events could be attributed to the overactive imaginations of some young residents.

During the press conference, officials suggested that the mysterious creature sighted by the couples might actually be a Sandhill Crane. Known for their impressive stature, Sandhill Cranes have long legs, a wingspan reaching up to six feet, and distinctly amber-red eyes that could appear darker under certain lighting conditions. These birds are common across many parts of North America, offering a plausible explanation for the sightings. The Sandhill Crane theory had previously been employed to demystify other folklore tales, including the Jersey Devil legend.

However, the Scarberrys and Mallettes remained firm in their description of the creature they encountered. They described a being with a human-like body, bat-like wings, and strikingly large red eyes that overshadowed its other facial features. They emphasized its extraordinary speed in flight and an awkward gait when on the ground.

On the night of the press conference, a group of armed locals ventured into the woods near the TNT area, intent on finding or hunting down this so-called Mothman. The local media, adopting a tone of light-hearted mockery, dubbed the creature "Mothman," likening it to a villain from the popular Adam West "Batman" TV series.

Despite Point Pleasant's efforts to downplay the situation, the unusual reports emanating from the area began drawing national attention. Among the intrigued was John Keel, a noted UFO-ologist and writer.

John Keel, years later, would recount his experiences in an interview with a youthful David Letterman. By the 1960s, Keel had made a name for himself as a writer fascinated by the bizarre and unexplained. A Korean War veteran, Keel was no stranger to confronting the unknown. His repertoire included a variety of outlandish and peculiar stories, and he had even penned teleplays for several 1960s TV shows.

Keel's interest in the UFO phenomenon, which was gaining momentum across the nation, eventually led him to Point Pleasant, West Virginia. This small town, now a hub of strange occurrences and sightings, had become a focal point for his research into the unexplained and extraordinary.

In the year following the initial Mothman sightings, John Keel engaged in extensive research, interviewing over a hundred individuals who claimed to have witnessed the enigmatic creature around Point Pleasant. The consistency in their accounts was striking: a large, man-like figure with an immense wingspan and intimidating red eyes that seemed to either hypnotize or terrify those who saw it.

One of the more chilling encounters took place just a day after the Scarberry and Mallette sighting, on November 16th. The event unfolded near the home of the Ralph Thomas family, located in proximity to the TNT area. That evening, a conspicuous red light appeared in the sky, capturing the attention of Marcella Bennett, a neighbor and friend of the Thomas family. Curious about the source of this eerie glow, Bennett drove to their house.

Her encounter with the Mothman was sudden and terrifying. As she reached to get her child from the backseat of her car, she was startled by a figure rising from the ground beside her. Bennett described it as a large, gray entity, taller than a man, with haunting glowing eyes.

Paralyzed with fear, Bennett momentarily dropped her child before recovering and rushing towards the safety of the Thomas family's house. Inside, both Bennett and the family witnessed the creature pacing around the patio and peering in through the windows with its glowing red eyes. The entity eventually left, but only after the arrival of the police.

The aftermath of this encounter was deeply traumatic for Marcella Bennett. She underwent months of therapy, struggling to cope with her day-to-day life, especially given her home's isolated location on the outskirts of Point Pleasant. Despite the severity of her trauma, many locals dismissed her story as part of an elaborate hoax, failing to acknowledge the real impact on her mental health.

However, Bennett was not alone in her experience. The Thomas family corroborated her account, reinforcing the credibility of what she had witnessed. Their testimony, along with Bennett's, joined the chorus of hundreds of other alleged witnesses to the Mothman, many of whom shared their encounters with Keel during his investigation.

John Keel's investigation in Point Pleasant extended over a year, delving deeply into the intertwining mysteries of the Mothman, UFO sightings, and a series of local animal mutilations. These elements collectively formed the core of his investigative writing.

In 1967, Keel became instrumental in popularizing the term "Men In Black," referring to mysterious figures purportedly associated with government agencies. These individuals were rumored to have visited Point Pleasant, adding another layer of intrigue to the ongoing events.

Keel himself started noticing strange occurrences that seemed to target those connected to the Mothman story. Mysterious alterations in mailed documents, disrupted phone lines, and a general sense of threat felt by UFO witnesses became frequent. Keel attributed these anomalies to the "Men In Black," theorizing that they were attempting to suppress the story and intimidate witnesses. This notion of shadowy figures trying to silence the truth became a persistent theme in the Mothman narrative.

During his time in Point Pleasant, Keel worked closely with Mary Hyre, a reporter for the Athens Messenger. Located in Athens, Ohio, about 40 miles north of Point Pleasant, the Athens Messenger had a sister publication in Point Pleasant, which facilitated Hyre's involvement in covering the Mothman phenomena. Unlike Keel, Hyre approached the story from a more localized and pragmatic standpoint, given her role in regional journalism.

By the latter half of 1967, public interest in the Mothman story began to wane, leading Keel to reduce his time in Point Pleasant. He made occasional visits for interviews with new witnesses but was no longer as present as he had been initially.

During one of his return trips, Keel was met by Mary Hyre, who shared a disturbing dream she had about people drowning amidst Christmas presents. While easily dismissible as a mere nightmare, Keel noted it, perhaps sensing its potential significance.

Back in New York, Keel himself started experiencing strange premonitions and claimed to receive telephonic messages from the enigmatic Indrid Cold, warning him to stay away from Point Pleasant. These messages, he believed, were ominous and significant.

Keel's absence from Point Pleasant in the final weeks of 1967 turned out to be fortuitous, as the town was about to face another significant and tragic event that would further cement its place in the annals of paranormal lore.

On the evening of December 15th, 1967, a catastrophic event shook Point Pleasant. During the busy rush hour, the Silver Bridge, a 700-foot structure spanning the Ohio River, suddenly collapsed. This tragic incident resulted in the loss of 46 lives, with two individuals never recovered, and numerous others sustaining injuries and psychological trauma. Interestingly, many of those affected by the collapse had reported witnessing the Mothman.

Built in 1928, the Silver Bridge had outlived its designed lifespan and had been subjected to much heavier traffic than it was intended to bear. The collapse underscored the critical importance of proper maintenance and safety in infrastructure.

In the aftermath of this disaster, media attention once again converged on Point Pleasant. Amidst the coverage, narratives linking the Mothman to the bridge collapse began to emerge. Some reports suggested that the Mothman had been seen on the day of the tragedy, leading to speculations that its presence was an ominous sign. However, after the bridge collapse, sightings of the Mothman in Point Pleasant ceased, as if its presence had vanished alongside the victims of the tragedy.

Yet, the strange occurrences in Point Pleasant didn't end with the bridge collapse. Mary Hyre, a reporter for the Athens Messenger who had been closely following the Mothman sightings, found herself inundated with reports of mysterious lights in the sky, which continued even after the bridge incident.

In one instance, she received an overwhelming number of calls—over 500 in a single weekend—reporting these unexplained lights.

One late evening in January 1968, Hyre had a disturbing encounter in her Point Pleasant courthouse office. A peculiar man, short in stature with a long-haired bowl cut and thick glasses, visited her. His presence and stuttering, low voice unnerved Hyre, especially since he showed an intense interest in the identities of those who had seen the lights in the sky. As he inched closer, Hyre felt increasingly threatened, eventually calling out for her boss. Before leaving abruptly, the man laughingly took a pen from her desk.

This mysterious visitor was rumored to have approached several residents in the area, all of whom had reported seeing the lights. Claiming to be a reporter from Ohio, yet seemingly ignorant about the region, he left a trail of discomfort and confusion before disappearing as mysteriously as he had arrived.

The Silver Bridge collapse irrevocably altered the essence of Point Pleasant. The once buoyant spirit of the 1960s, fueled by UFO excitement, was over-shadowed by a more somber symbol: the Mothman, an emblem of foreboding and tragedy.

In the years that followed, the Mothman transcended from a local curiosity to an urban legend, a harbinger of doom in popular folklore. The 1971 investiga-tion into the bridge disaster pinpointed a minor flaw in the suspension eyebar as the catastrophic trigger. This discovery led to nationwide revisions in infrastructure maintenance standards, highlighting the far-reaching impact of the tragedy.

John Keel's 1975 book, "The Mothman Prophecies," reignited interest in the Mothman narrative. His account, chronicling his own psychological journey amidst the bizarre events of 1966 and 1967, has been both lauded and criticized. The book, while a key reference for Mothman enthusiasts, demands a reader willing to entertain the far-fetched and unexplained.

Point Pleasant gradually healed from the profound grief of losing many community members but remained indelibly marked by the events. The town, reclaiming its identity from the grip of paranormal lore, embraced the Mothman legend, with local museums and stores featuring related memorabilia.

In 2002, coinciding with the release of "The Mothman Prophecies" film starring Richard Gere, Point Pleasant initiated the annual Mothman Festival. This event, celebrating the legend, coincided with the movie's dramatized depiction of the Silver Bridge collapse, contributing modestly to its cultural footprint.

The Mothman legend persisted, weaving its way into West Virginia's cultural tapestry. It has been linked to other disasters globally, such as the Chernobyl Blackbird sighting prior to the nuclear meltdown. However, the existence of the Mothman and Indrid Cold remains unverified, leaving this story perpetually enigmatic and unresolved in the annals of folklore and mystery.

Murder of Jennifer Lockmiller

J ennifer Lockmiller's life story is a remarkable tapestry of talent, resilience, and passion, woven from her earliest days in Decatur, Illinois, to her promising years as a journalism student. Born on January 11, 1971, to Richard and Norma Lockmiller, Jennifer was the cherished youngest sibling in a family of five and the only daughter. Her early years in this bustling household set the stage for a life marked by both achievements and challenges.

Jennifer shone brightly as a student, graduating with honors from Eisenhower High School in Decatur in 1989. Her academic journey then took her to Illinois Wesleyan College (IWU) in Bloomington, followed by a transfer to Illinois State University (ISU) in Normal in 1992, where she pursued her passion for journalism. These years were pivotal, shaping Jennifer's identity as a scholar and a budding journalist.

From an incredibly young age, Jennifer displayed an insatiable thirst for knowledge. By the tender age of 3 1/2, she had already taught herself to read, a skill she acquired by keenly watching the children's television show "Electric Company." This early achievement was a harbinger of the brilliance that defined her.

Jennifer's artistic side was equally remarkable. Between the ages of seven and fourteen, she honed her musical talents through piano studies at Millikin University's preparatory program. Her recitals were a testament to her dedication and skill, earning admiration from all who heard her play.

However, Jennifer's journey was not without its hurdles. During her freshman year of high school, what began as an innocent desire to lose a few pounds spiraled into a struggle with Anorexia Nervosa. This eating disorder became a significant challenge, leading to multiple hospitalizations. Yet, in the face of adversity, Jennifer found strength and purpose. Together with her mother, Norma, she founded a local chapter of a national support group for the eating disorder, turning her personal battle into a crusade to help others.

During her time at IWU, Jennifer faced a relapse, but with medication and support, she emerged stronger. By the time she transferred to ISU, she had triumphantly overcome her illness, a testament to her resilience and determination.

Music was a constant source of joy for Jennifer, with a particular fondness for The Beatles. She even named the family dog Abbey, a nod to the iconic Beatles album, "Abbey Road." But it was her love for writing that truly captured her soul. At ISU, she joined "The Daily Vidette" as a student journalist, a role that allowed her to channel her creativity and insights into words.

Jennifer Lockmiller's life was a blend of bright promise and profound challenges, marked by her extraordinary intellect, artistic talent, and courageous fight against personal demons. Her future, full of potential and hope, was tragically cut short on a summer day, leaving behind a legacy of inspiration and a story that continues to touch hearts.

The mysterious and tragic case of Jennifer Lockmiller's death unfolds like a dark, intricate puzzle, leaving more questions than answers in its wake. It all began on a seemingly ordinary day in Normal, Illinois, but what unfolded would forever change the lives of those who knew Jennifer.

On August 28, 1993, Morgan Keefe, a close friend of 22-year-old Jennifer Lockmiller, felt a growing sense of unease. Jennifer had fallen off the radar for a few days, which was uncharacteristic of her. Driven by concern, Morgan decided to check on her at her apartment at 412 N. Main Street. What she discovered upon entering Jennifer's home at around 2:10 p.m. was a scene that would haunt her forever. The door, surprisingly unlocked, led Morgan to a horrifying sight – Jennifer lay lifeless, a pair of scissors protruding ominously from her chest, and a ligature, which was later identified as the cord from her alarm clock, was wrapped tightly around her neck. The chilling scene also suggested a sexual assault, adding a layer of brutality to the already gruesome scene.

The police, promptly called to the scene by a distraught Morgan, arrived to find the apartment eerily undisturbed. There were no signs of a struggle, no evidence of forced entry – a sinister indication that Jennifer might have known her assailant.

The subsequent investigation by Normal police was a whirlwind of leads and dead ends. Among the most puzzling clues were the fingerprints found on the alarm clock cord used to strangle Jennifer. Three distinct sets were identified: one belonging to Michael Swaine, Jennifer's current boyfriend; another to Alan Beaman, her ex-boyfriend who once shared a room with Michael; and a third set, frustratingly unidentifiable. Adding to the complexity, _The Pantagraph_ reported that Michael had moved in with Jennifer just days before her murder.

Both Michael and Alan were immediately questioned in the aftermath of the killing. Despite the tense and emotional interrogations, neither man was charged. The Pantagraph noted a particularly dramatic moment when one of the men – it's unclear whether it was Michael or Alan – was handcuffed and taken away, more due to his agitated state than being a suspect.

The investigation extended to Jennifer's car, where police searched for any clue that might shed light on the case. However, the outcome of this examination remains unclear.

Two months after the tragic incident, the police made a startling announcement. A prime suspect had emerged, though their identity was shrouded in secrecy. Alongside this revelation, a $10,000 reward was offered for information leading to the resolution of this perplexing case. The suspect, according to authorities, possessed both the means and the motive for the murder.

The enigmatic circumstances surrounding Jennifer Lockmiller's murder unfolded against a backdrop of her ambitious journalistic pursuits at Illinois State University's newspaper, _The Daily Vidette_. Jennifer, brimming with the enthusiasm of a dedicated journalism student, had embarked on her first assignment of the school year, a potentially incisive story about the Normal Police Department. Her mother, Norma, aware of the sensitive nature of such investigations, cautioned her with a prescient warning: "Because you never know when you might need their help." This cryptic advice lingered in the air, unexplored but laden with significance. Why did Norma feel compelled to issue such a warning? What underlying concerns might have prompted this maternal advice?

In the tangled web of this case, a significant development occurred on May 17, 1994. Alan Beaman, a 21-year-old theater major at Illinois Wesleyan University (IWU) and Jennifer's ex-boyfriend, was arrested for her murder. Alan and Jennifer's relationship, which had blossomed and then withered over several months, had ended in March 1993. Their love story, marred by tumultuous breakups and reconciliations, was a roller coaster of emotions.

Alan, hailing from Rockford, Illinois – a city about two hours north of Normal – was described by acquaintances as someone incapable of murder. They painted a picture of a warm, gentle, and kind individual, albeit tinged with frustration. However, the police narrative starkly contrasted this image. Interviews with Jennifer's friends and family revealed a different side of Alan – one marked by jealousy, especially towards Jennifer's other romantic interests, and a temper that seemed at odds with his otherwise amiable demeanor.

Disturbing allegations surfaced about Alan's behavior. It was claimed that he had once broken doors to Jennifer's apartment and that Jennifer had resorted to barricading her door with chairs to keep him out. In one extreme instance, a friend had even used mace to force him to leave.

The couple's relationship was characterized by its volatility – they had reportedly broken up around 18 times, oscillating between intense arguments and passionate reconciliations, sometimes even discussing engagement.

Police, focusing on Alan, pointed to the motive and physical evidence – notably, his fingerprints on the alarm clock cord used in the murder. Arresting him as he exited a final exam, they charged him with Jennifer's murder. From the outset, Alan vehemently maintained his innocence, providing an alibi that he was in Rockford at the time of the murder. Despite this, the police hypothesized that he could have made the four-hour round trip from Rockford to Normal to commit the crime. This theory persisted even in the face of witnesses who corroborated Alan's presence in Rockford.

As the case against Alan Beaman proceeded, it raised questions about motive, opportunity, and the veracity of alibis. The narrative of a conflicted lover, a concerned mother's warning, and a police department under scrutiny coalesced into a complex and compelling story that continued to unfold, challenging perceptions of truth and justice in the search for answers to Jennifer Lockmiller's tragic death.

The trial of Alan Beaman, which began in 1995, was a dramatic and emotionally charged event that captivated public attention. Alan's behavior during the trial did little to garner sympathy from the court or the public. His demeanor was often perceived as unemotional and arrogant, and his frequent smiles at reporters gave the impression of someone who relished the spotlight, rather than a defendant grappling with serious charges.

A pivotal moment in the trial came with the testimony of Michael Swaine, a key witness for the prosecution. Michael, who was Alan's former roommate and Jennifer Lockmiller's boyfriend at the time of her murder, provided a narrative that painted a picture of jealousy and anger. He described the evolution of his relationship with Jennifer, detailing how their connection grew and ultimately led to a romantic involvement. This development, according to Michael, deeply affected Alan, who was still in a relationship with Jennifer at the time.

Michael recounted a significant episode that occurred on June 11, 1993. He and Jennifer shared a kiss, an act that led them to the Sigma Chi fraternity house, still under construction. There, in the secrecy of the basement, they initiated a physical relationship. Michael testified that they had been intimate several times, with their last encounter occurring just a week before Jennifer's tragic murder.

The tension between Alan and Michael was palpable. Michael described a tense encounter where Alan, fueled by suspicion and jealousy, arrived at Jennifer's apartment while Michael was consoling her. In a panic, Michael hid in the closet under a pile of clothes. He recounted how Alan, in a frenzied state, searched the apartment, including the closet and even Jennifer's bathroom garbage can, possibly looking for evidence of birth control.

The police, however, ruled Michael out as a suspect. His alibi was solid; he was working in Elmhurst and staying with his parents during the estimated time frame of Jennifer's murder.

The trial also shed light on the nature of the relationship between Alan and Jennifer, particularly through the letters Alan had written to her. These letters varied in content, some detailing sexual fantasies, while others expressed anger and frustration over their breakup.

The culmination of the trial in April 1995 was a watershed moment. Alan Beaman was found guilty and, in May 1995, sentenced to 50 years in prison.

This verdict, however, was not the end of the story. It was merely a chapter in a complex and evolving narrative, one that continued to unfold, raising questions about justice, truth, and the intricacies of human relationships.

The saga of Alan Beaman, convicted in 1995 for the murder of his ex-girlfriend Jennifer Lockmiller, took a dramatic turn 13 years later when the highest court in Illinois overturned his conviction, sparking a reexamination of a case that had once seemed closed.

The court's decision was rooted in a violation of Beaman's constitutional rights to due process. The judges highlighted the absence of crucial evidence during the original trial that could have potentially exonerated Beaman. This groundbreaking ruling called for a new trial, upending years of perceived judicial certainty.

The core of Beaman's defense, as argued by his lawyer, Karen Daniel, hinged on two vital points. Firstly, the jury in the initial trial was not presented with evidence that could have categorically ruled out Beaman as a suspect. Secondly, there was another potential suspect, known enigmatically as "John Doe", who had been romantically involved with Jennifer. This individual, who lived a mere two miles from Jennifer, had a troubling history of domestic battery and was known to have provided her with drugs. Significantly, "John Doe" had also claimed that Jennifer owed him money. This information, including the fact that "John Doe" had failed a polygraph test, was not disclosed during the trial, a critical omission that called the integrity of the conviction into question.

During the appeal process, the timeline of Beaman's activities on the day of Jennifer's murder was scrutinized. A bank receipt confirmed his presence in Rockford at 10:11 a.m. that day. Further, two phone calls from Beaman's home in Rockford to a church he attended cast doubts on the prosecution's theory that he could have traveled to Normal, committed the murder, and returned before his mother came home from shopping. The lack of conclusive evidence about his whereabouts at the time of the murder remained a complicating factor.

In the years that followed, the case took several more twists. In January 2009, all charges against Beaman were dropped. Subsequent DNA testing in 2012 revealed two unknown male DNA profiles, ruling out Beaman and three other previously considered suspects. In 2013, Judge Jeffrey Ford granted Beaman a certificate of innocence and awarded him state compensation. Despite these developments, Beaman's attempts at legal redress through federal and county lawsuits faced hurdles, with initial dismissals eventually leading to the Illinois Supreme Court remanding his case for further proceedings in 2019.

The dramatic turn of events culminated in January 2015 when then–Governor Pat Quinn pardoned Beaman based on actual innocence. In 2018, a phone tip prompted the Normal police to reopen the case.

As of March 2023, there was a possibility that Beaman's case could return to a McLean County judge. Amidst these legal battles, the haunting question remains: Who killed Jennifer Lockmiller? The enigmatic "John Doe" lingers in the background of this mystery, his whereabouts and role in the case still shrouded in uncertainty. Questions about the police's singular focus on Beaman and the overlooked leads continue to fuel debates and investigations. The quest for truth in the tragic death of Jennifer Lockmiller persists, a reminder of the complexities and imperfections of the justice system.

Murder of Arlis Perry

On a crisp autumn evening in Palo Alto, California, October 12th, 1974, the air was still warm with the remnants of summer. The Saturday night was calm, the kind that would be perfect for a leisurely stroll through the streets, a common activity among locals and visitors alike.

In this serene setting, a security guard at Stanford University was working the overnight shift. It was a typical Saturday night, with most people either indulging in the vibrant college lifestyle or enjoying a quiet night in, possibly celebrating the Stanford Cardinals' recent 13-13 tie in a football game, a highlight in an otherwise disappointing season.

On such a night, a security guard, tasked with patrolling the campus, might find it challenging to maintain a high level of dedication to the job. The allure of the weekend could make even the most diligent worker long to be elsewhere, leading to a somewhat relaxed approach to their duties. This might involve rushing through certain parts of the security rounds or not paying full attention to every detail. In some cases, a guard who's less committed might even consider skipping certain tasks, justifying it with the belief that nothing unusual is likely to happen.

This could have been the scenario for Stephen Crawford, a security guard at the university. Possibly feeling a mix of fatigue, frustration, and boredom from working on the weekend, he might have been inclined to take shortcuts in his duties. Having held the position for a considerable time, he might have developed a sense of complacency, assured by the routine nature of his job and the belief that the campus was a safe and uneventful place.

However, as the shift was nearing its end, and during one of the final rounds, an unexpected discovery was made. This event, far from being ordinary, had the potential to alter the course of the guard's life, challenging the perceived safety and predictability of the university campus.

Bruce Perry and Arlis Dykema, both hailing from the tranquil town of Bismarck, North Dakota, shared a quintessential American story. Their paths crossed at Bismarck High School, a meeting that marked the beginning of a deep connection.

Their relationship mirrored the classic American high school romance. Bruce, a versatile student, excelled both academically and athletically, making a name for himself in track and field while also achieving scholarly success. Arlis, embodying the traits of a traditional cheerleader, combined her conservative, religious values with her intelligence and kindness.

Despite the challenges posed by Bruce's acceptance to Stanford University, over 1500 miles away, the couple decided to maintain their relationship. The year was 1974, and long-distance communication was a game of patience, relying on landlines and handwritten letters, a stark contrast to the convenience of modern technology.

At Stanford, Bruce faced the demanding life of a pre-med student, juggling academic responsibilities with the complexities of a long-distance relationship, a formidable challenge for anyone, let alone someone adapting to an environment vastly different from North Dakota. California in 1974, especially around Palo Alto, was a melting pot of new ideas and cultures, diverging significantly from the conservative backdrop of his hometown.

Meanwhile, Arlis, back in North Dakota, was equally busy. After graduating high school, she enrolled in Bismarck Junior College and worked at a dental office, all while being deeply involved in her church activities. Her commitment to Christianity was evident in her work with various church organizations, including Young Life and the Fellowship of Christian Athletes.

The distance and their individual commitments took a toll on their relationship, leading to a mutual decision that would change their lives: marriage. In the summer of 1974, they celebrated their union at Bismarck Reformed Church on August 17th, an event marking the beginning of a new chapter together.

Following a brief honeymoon in a cabin owned by Arlis' parents, the couple embarked on their journey to California. There, they were set to start their life together, embracing the new opportunities and challenges that awaited them.

Bruce and Arlis Perry, now united in matrimony, settled into an apartment in Quillen Hall, a space designated for married couples at Stanford University. The apartment was modest, yet they began transforming it into their cozy abode. Shortly after their wedding, Bruce dove back into his rigorous pre-med studies, dedicating most of his time to classes, studying, and test preparations. Meanwhile, Arlis, initially focusing on her role as a homemaker, soon found employment as a receptionist at a law firm in Palo Alto.

Arlis often spent her free hours exploring the Stanford campus, where she discovered the Stanford Memorial Church. The grandeur and beauty of this church captivated her, becoming a place she frequented. It's easy to understand her fascination, as the church's impressive architecture is quite striking.

However, Arlis experienced a sense of isolation following the move. In her correspondence with family and friends back in North Dakota, she expressed feelings of loneliness. She wrote about the challenge of finding friends in this new environment, contemplating reaching out to strangers in her quest for companionship. Despite this, she remained hopeful, trusting in her faith and the strength of her relationship with Bruce to navigate these challenges.

Arlis also shared her enthusiasm for the Californian weather and her new job in her letters. These elements were bright spots in her life, signaling that things were beginning to settle for the couple in their new surroundings.

On October 12th, the Stanford campus was immersed in its usual weekend rhythm. The football team, once a beacon of pride, was grappling with a challenging season, having just tied their second game against UCLA. The campus was buzzing with students, some engaged in typical college festivities, yet an overall calm pervaded the evening. As the season transitioned from summer to fall, it was a fitting night for a walk, a decision Arlis made, with Bruce joining her, setting aside his medical studies for a brief respite.

Their walk led them towards a distant mailbox, where Arlis intended to post letters to her family in North Dakota. Although the mail wouldn't be collected until Monday, Bruce saw this as an opportunity for the couple to spend time together. However, during their walk, a seemingly trivial argument erupted between them, a common occurrence in any relationship. The subject of the dispute, who should refill their vehicle's air, might seem trivial, but such minor disagreements are often part of married life.

As the argument neared its end, near the Stanford Memorial Church, a frequent haunt for Arlis, she requested some time alone. Bruce, understanding the need for space, headed back to their apartment in Quillen Hall. Arlis, meanwhile, entered the church to pray. Inside, two other individuals briefly noticed her presence before leaving.

These two individuals, while exiting the church, observed a young man entering. He appeared to be in his mid-twenties, with sandy blond hair and a medium build, wearing a short-sleeved blue shirt. His youthful appearance was the only detail that stood out to them.

Back at their apartment, Bruce anticipated resuming their discussion upon Arlis's return. However, unbeknownst to him, a sinister turn of events was beginning to unfold, changing the course of the night dramatically.

On the night of October 12th, 1974, Stephen was on duty. His responsibilities included ensuring that campus buildings, including the Stanford Memorial Church, were securely closed and locked at appropriate times. Arlis Perry visited the church that night, and it was Stephen's task to lock up the church after its closing time at midnight, which coincided closely with the last time Arlis was seen by two witnesses.

Stephen reported that he entered the church shortly after midnight, announcing the closure and asking anyone present to leave. He noted that the time was approximately 12:10 AM when he made this announcement. Despite this, he did not see anyone inside the church, including Arlis, the earlier witnesses, or the young man with sandy hair who was observed entering the church. Following his routine, Stephen then secured the church, leaving the building unaware of the unfolding events inside.

Bruce Perry waited anxiously at their apartment for his wife Arlis to return from her solitary time at the church. Living only half a mile away, he started to worry when she hadn't returned by 12:15 AM.

Feeling uneasy, Bruce left their apartment to search for Arlis. He reached the Stanford Memorial Church, only to find it securely locked, with no sign of her around the building. Bruce expanded his search across the campus, knowing that Arlis, new to California, had neither friends nor family nearby to visit. Given her conservative nature, it seemed unlikely she would be at a party. He checked their usual walking route home, hoping to either find her or that she had returned to the apartment.

Meanwhile, a passerby near the church later reported hearing an unusual sound, but at the time, it didn't raise immediate alarm. Bruce's search, however, led him back to an empty apartment. He began to hope that Arlis had either taken an extended walk to cool off or had accidentally fallen asleep in the church and would return soon.

Around 2 AM, Stephen Crawford, the security guard, was on another patrol around the campus. His duties included checking the church for any stragglers. He found the doors still locked and reported no signs of activity.

By 3 AM, with Arlis still missing, Bruce decided to call the police. He expressed concern that she might have inadvertently been locked inside the church. Responding to his call, Stanford security officers found the church doors locked and assumed it was unlikely anyone was inside. Due to the church's size and the inability to see inside, they didn't investigate further.

Early in the morning, around 5:30 AM, Stephen Crawford was conducting his routine campus patrol. While passing the Memorial Church, he noticed something unusual: a side door was open. It appeared to have been forced from the inside, a detail that would later spark various theories about the events of the night.

Crawford, upon discovering the open door, cautiously entered the church. He observed that the altar and its surroundings were undisturbed, suggesting that nothing valuable had been taken. This might have led him to initially think the situation was not grave, perhaps attributing it to students seeking a secluded spot.

However, his investigation took a grim turn when he reached the front pews on the left side of the church, the same area where Arlis Perry had last been seen. There, he made a horrifying discovery: the body of Arlis Perry. She was found in a shocking state, with her lower garments removed and arranged in a disturbing manner.

The evidence of the brutality Arlis faced was clear. She had been subjected to severe beating and strangulation. More chillingly, an ice pick had been driven into her skull, suggesting premeditation by the perpetrator. The violence did not stop there; her body was manipulated post-mortem in a grotesque display. Her blouse was torn, and her arms were positioned to hold an altar candle, placed in a macabre manner. Additionally, a large candle had been inserted into her body, a final act of desecration.

Crawford, deeply shaken by this discovery, immediately alerted the authorities. The Santa Clara Sheriff's Department, which had jurisdiction over Stanford University, was called to the scene.

As police and detectives arrived, the scheduled Sunday mass had to be relocated to a different part of the church. Reverend Robert Hammerton-Kelly, who witnessed the crime scene, described it as having ritualistic and satanic elements. Despite the grim circumstances, he insisted on proceeding with the mass, determined not to let such evil overshadow their faith.

In criminal investigations, the process often starts close to the victim, examining those in their immediate circle before expanding outward. Following this approach, the police first visited Bruce Perry at the couple's residence in Quillen Hall soon after Arlis Perry's tragic death.

Upon their arrival, the officers found Bruce Perry in a state that initially raised suspicions: he was covered in blood. This detail, as mentioned in Maury Terry's book "The Ultimate Evil," led the detectives who visited the apartment to consider detaining Perry immediately. The sight of him covered in blood, combined with the recent brutal murder of his wife, seemed incriminating.

However, it turned out that the blood on Perry was his own. He explained that he suffered from stress-induced nosebleeds, a condition that is not uncommon. Given the timing of the event in mid-October, with seasonal changes, such a reaction seemed plausible.

Despite the initial suspicion due to Perry's appearance and the relatively short duration of their marriage, the investigation did not find substantial evidence linking him to the crime. The blood on Perry was tested and confirmed to match his type, which was presumably different from Arlis Perry's. Furthermore, Perry also passed a polygraph test. Though the reliability of polygraph tests is now questioned, back in 1974, they were considered highly credible by criminal investigators, leading them to rule out Bruce Perry as a suspect.

The detectives then shifted their focus towards identifying a suspect with a history of sexual deviancy or related criminal activities. Although there was no evidence to suggest that Arlis Perry had been raped, the circumstances of her death, particularly the candle found inside her body and a church pillow nearby with semen on it, pointed towards a sexually motivated crime.

The investigation also involved analyzing a palm print found on the candle. This print did not match either Bruce Perry or Stephen Crawford, the security guard who discovered the body.

Authorities estimated that Arlis had been killed around midnight. This timeline cast doubt on security guard Stephen Crawford's claim that he had conducted a sweep of the Memorial Church after 2:00 AM. If Crawford had indeed checked the church at that time, it suggested that Arlis was either still alive and concealed by her assailant, or that the crime had already occurred and was missed during the inspection.

This led to a chilling hypothesis: the perpetrator might have executed the murder in a slow, deliberate manner. Arlis could have been in the church, hearing Crawford's patrol and perhaps even her husband Bruce's calls for her after midnight.

Investigators discovered that the side door Crawford found open had been forced from the inside. This suggested that the killer might have remained hidden in the church for several hours, possibly until the security officers arrived in response to Bruce Perry's 911 call at 3:00 AM, then made an escape.

The prolonged nature of these events implied that Arlis endured a significant ordeal before her death. Given that she was new to the area and knew very few people besides her husband, the motive and identity of her attacker remained a deeply troubling mystery.

A memorial service for Arlis was held a few days after her murder, poignantly in the same Stanford Memorial Church where she was found. Bruce Perry and his family attended, surrounded by the stark reminder of the tragedy that had taken place.

Arlis, having been in California for a brief period, had not formed local connections, so most attendees did not know her personally. Another service was planned in her hometown of Bismarck.

However, a revelation came during the Stanford service. A coworker of Arlis from the Palo Alto law firm attended and was surprised to see Bruce Perry, mistaking him for another man he had seen with Arlis. This coworker shared that Arlis had started at the firm just two weeks before her death and had kept her work life separate from her personal life, with Bruce not visiting her at work.

Interestingly, the coworker described a visit by a young man on October 11th, the day before Arlis's murder. The man, with blond hair and a stocky build, appeared to have a serious conversation with Arlis, lasting about fifteen minutes.

Despite the coworker's description aligning with the young man seen entering the church on the night of Arlis's murder, the investigation did not extensively pursue this lead. Perhaps the description was too common among the 1970s Palo Alto population, particularly at Stanford, making it challenging to pinpoint a specific individual.

Decades later, the case remains unsolved, with this potential lead and other details still shrouded in uncertainty, leaving unanswered questions in a tragic and open case.

Less than a week after her tragic death, Arlis Perry was returned to her hometown of Bismarck, North Dakota, where her funeral was held at the Bismarck Reformed Church. This was the same place where she had married Bruce Perry not long before. Understandably, her friends and family were devastated. Their daughter, a young woman committed to her faith and family, had been gruesomely murdered within months of leaving home.

Initially, the gruesome details of Arlis's murder were not public knowledge. Her family and friends only knew she had been killed, spared, for a time, the knowledge of the more horrific aspects of her death.

Arlis was laid to rest in a local cemetery in Bismarck, a place she had always considered home. While her burial allowed some semblance of closure for her loved ones, many questions about her murder remained unanswered.

Around Halloween, less than two weeks after Arlis's funeral, a temporary grave marker at her burial site was stolen. This act was seen as both heartless and highly suspicious. Some speculated that the theft indicated the involvement of someone from Bismarck, as only Arlis's grave was disturbed. This led to theories that her killer might have taken the marker as a morbid trophy.

These suspicions were somewhat supported by the Santa Clara detectives' revelation that personal items of Arlis had been taken from the crime scene. However, the theory that her killer was from Bismarck and had followed her to California seemed far-fetched. Tracking her across such a distance would have been a considerable and conspicuous undertaking.

Criticism has been levied over the years at the detectives for not pursuing leads in Bismarck more vigorously. While it seems unlikely, the possibility that the killer originated from Arlis's hometown and followed her to Stanford cannot be entirely dismissed.

In Maury Terry's book "The Ultimate Evil," a rumor is mentioned, allegedly started by Bruce Perry's parents, about Arlis reaching out to Satanic cultists in Bismarck in the year before moving to California. Terry theorized that these cultists might have tracked her down to perform a ritualistic killing. However, this theory, which emerged during the peak of the Satanic Panic in the United States, lacks substantial evidence and seems implausible.

Terry's book also ties the murder to a supposed nationwide Satanic cult, alleging connections to serial killers like David Berkowitz (Son of Sam) and Charles Manson. However, these connections are tenuous, mainly based on Berkowitz's claims made after his arrest for the Son of Sam murders. Berkowitz, known for sending provocative letters and stirring controversy, later claimed involvement in a cult responsible for various crimes, including Arlis's murder.

While these claims made headlines, they have been widely discredited by FBI investigators, psychologists, and forensic experts. Berkowitz's later allegations are generally seen as fantasies, likely concocted during his long imprisonment.

Murders of Andrew and Patricia Puskas

In the quaint town of New Brunswick, New Jersey, a love story unfolded between Andrew Richard Puskas and Patricia Nodes, culminating in a beautiful wedding on May 4, 1968, at St. Mary of Mount Virgin R.C. Church. Their journey together began as classmates at New Brunswick High School, graduating in 1964. Andrew pursued further education at Trenton State College and Union County Technical Institute, earning an associate degree. His sense of duty led him to serve in the United States Army Special Forces, a testament to his character and resilience.

Patricia, sharing a similar educational path, also attended the prestigious St. Mary's School in New Brunswick and Linwood School in North Brunswick. Together, they embarked on a life filled with love, faith, and family, becoming proud parents to Andrew Junior, aged 9, Scott, 7, and Brian, 3.

The Puskas family, always seeking growth and community, moved to Piscataway, embracing the teachings of Jehovah's Witnesses. Their spiritual journey continued, and in 1974, they settled at 182 First Street in the borough of Middlesex. Their involvement with the Middlesex Bible Church began in 1977, sparked by sending their children to the church's vacation Bible school. This marked the beginning of a deep and fulfilling relationship with the church community.

Andrew, at 35, found his calling as a technical service representative at Dodge Newark Supply Inc. in Fairfield, a role he held since 1975. Patricia, also 35, dedicated her time to nurturing their family and faith. Their lives were deeply intertwined with the Middlesex Bible Church, where they were active and cherished members. Andrew and Patricia's commitment to their faith was evident in their weekly activities; Tuesdays were for Bible study, Fridays saw Andrew leading a teen Bible study group, and Saturdays were reserved for religious film screenings at the church. Patricia's Sundays were spent teaching a class of six- and seven-year-olds, sharing her faith and wisdom.

Andrew's devotion extended to his role as a lay minister at the church, and he was on the path to becoming the church's fourth elder, as noted by elder Raymond Good.

On the frosty morning of February 25, 1982, in the quiet neighborhood of Middlesex, New Jersey, Andrew Puskas experienced a day that would forever be etched in the town's memory. As he readied his two older sons, Andrew Jr. and Scott, for school, a seemingly innocuous package on his front porch caught his attention. Little did he know that this discovery would soon turn their peaceful life upside down.

Andrew, sensing something amiss with the package, instinctively sent his boys outside, prioritizing their safety. His quick thinking led him to call the police, unknowingly setting in motion a series of events that would shake the community to its core.

Responding to the call, Sgt. Benson immediately radioed Officer Richard Schwarz, a young and dedicated officer patrolling just a block away. Schwarz, at 24, was the epitome of a committed policeman, but he struggled to locate the Puskas residence in the winding streets of Middlesex. This minor delay, which he initially thought of as an inconvenience, turned out to be a lifesaving twist of fate.

As Officer Schwarz approached the Puskas home, about to step onto the front porch, the unthinkable happened. The house exploded with such force that it sent him flying over the hood of his patrol car, a mere 30 feet from the epicenter of the blast. The explosion, a monstrous roar heard throughout the neighborhood, lifted the roof off the one-story frame home and violently blew out the front door.

In the midst of chaos and confusion, Officer Schwarz, though shaken, demonstrated remarkable bravery. He lunged for his police radio, his voice urgent but clear, calling for immediate assistance: "Send everybody!" His call to action was not just professional duty but a personal crusade to save lives.

Miraculously, Andrew Jr. and Scott, who were blown off the front porch by the blast, only suffered minor injuries. Their younger brother, Brian, sat unscathed in the car, waiting for a father who would never return. Officer Schwarz, embodying the spirit of a true hero, rushed to smother the flames engulfing the children, ensuring their safety amidst the chaos.

The aftermath of the explosion revealed a scene of devastation. The Puskas home was partially destroyed, its debris scattered, and neighboring houses, including the one at 176 First Street, were damaged. It took authorities four grueling hours to extract the bodies of Andrew and Patricia from the collapsed kitchen floor, a heartbreaking end to a family's story.

The two older boys, scarred but alive, were taken to Green Brook Regional Center for treatment of their burns. The Chief County Medical Examiner, Dr. Marvin Schuster, conducted autopsies that revealed shrapnel in the victims' abdomen and chest, indicating they faced the explosion. The autopsy reports concluded that both Andrew and Patricia succumbed to "traumatic and hemorrhagic shock due to explosion," a stark reminder of the fragility of life.

In the aftermath of the tragic explosion at the Puskas residence, a young witness provided the police with crucial details. The child meticulously described the contents of a mysterious package: a 2-foot-square, unmarked cardboard box. Inside, it harbored a perilous assembly of several bottles and a pipe bomb, ominously equipped with a 45-second timer. This chilling account, as recounted by Del Vecchio in 1982, was a pivotal piece in unraveling the harrowing event.

The Middlesex County Crime Stoppers page offered a more detailed description of the contents. Among the items, two bottles stood out for their distinct hues of blue – one a deep, dark blue and the other a lighter shade. The most significant clue emerged from a fragment of glass found at the crime scene, bearing the partial molded inscription "KING'S." This piece of evidence hinted at a potential lead in the investigation.

Further examination revealed that the bottles contained a flammable liquid, believed by some reports to be gasoline. This discovery suggested a premeditated and malicious intent behind the creation of the explosive device.

Addressed specifically to Andrew Richard Puskas, the package's labeling was a curious detail. In his professional life, Andrew was known as "Andy," while his friends and church members affectionately called him "Dick." The way the package was addressed could offer a significant clue about the sender's relationship with Andrew and their familiarity with his personal life.

As the investigation deepened, it became evident that the package was personally placed on the front porch by the perpetrator, rather than being sent through conventional means like the United States Postal Service or a shipping carrier like United Parcel Service (UPS).

Investigators conducted extensive interviews with friends, neighbors, and members of the Middlesex Bible Church, seeking any hint of a motive for this heinous act. However, nothing in the couple's background or interactions raised any suspicions or provided a clear reason for such a targeted attack.

Andrew's colleagues at work were also interviewed, but these inquiries led to dead ends. The prevailing theory among investigators was that this act of violence stemmed from "personal hatred" towards Andrew Puskas.

In their quest for answers, investigators sent several large sacks filled with debris from the explosion site to the Bureau of Alcohol, Tobacco (ATF), and Firearms lab in Rockville, Maryland. This evidence included samples of wood, human tissue, and water from firefighting efforts, all in the hope of uncovering clues about the bomb's nature. After weeks of analysis, some evidence emerged, but it was not disclosed in further detail.

The ATF's examination concluded that the bomb was a "fairly sophisticated device," as noted by then-ATF agent Johnny Bouras. This finding ruled out the possibility of a remote-controlled detonation, pointing towards a more direct and calculated approach in the bomb's design and placement.

In the aftermath of the tragedy, a 17-year-old girl's observation added a new dimension to the investigation. She vividly remembered a white Mercury Cougar making a hasty and abrupt stop at the end of First Street, before swiftly turning west onto Union Avenue (Route 28). Her keen eye noted two white males inside the vehicle, though the fleeting moment didn't allow her to catch the license plate number. This detail, although seemingly minor, hinted at a potential getaway vehicle and suspects, adding layers to the already complex case.

In the immediate aftermath of the blast, a neighbor, drawn by the commotion, witnessed a heart-wrenching scene. The Puskas children were in a state of shock and confusion, frantically running around. Amidst their panic, she heard one of them utter a chilling statement: "My parents are in there. I knew they were out to get us." However, this account took an unexpected turn when the neighbor later retracted her story, and the children denied making such a remark, casting a shroud of mystery over the events following the explosion.

Several months later, in June 1982, another neighbor stepped forward with a crucial piece of information. On the fateful day of the explosion, she was delayed in her routine, which led her to observe a suspicious vehicle near the Puskas residence just before the ominous package was discovered.

Under hypnosis, the woman provided a more detailed account. She recalled a late-model, mid-sized white station wagon, which seemed out of place, either pulling into the Puskas' driveway or the adjacent property. As she prepared to leave her own driveway, the car caught her attention as it passed by, and once again, it appeared in her rearview mirror as she drove away.

Her description of the driver was quite specific: a white male, likely in his late 40s or early 50s, with an average build, standing about 5 feet 8 to 5 feet 10 inches tall. He had an olive complexion, dark eyes, bushy eyebrows, and dark hair peppered with specks of gray. An intriguing detail was a rectangular sign on the vehicle's passenger door – a white background with a red border, featuring a capital letter 'S' or 'C' followed by smaller red, cursive letters.

Though she couldn't recall the license plate's letters or numbers, she believed it to be straw-colored, similar to the New Jersey license plates issued between 1959 and 1977. Additionally, she remembered seeing a box in the back of the car, which could be linked to the deadly package left at the Puskas home.

In an effort to solidify this crucial testimony, the woman worked with a sketch artist from the Middlesex County Sheriff's Office. Together, they created a composite sketch based on her detailed recollection, hoping it would bring them closer to solving the enigmatic and tragic case that had befallen the Puskas family.

As the investigation progressed into April 1982, it began to lose its initial intensity. Despite interviewing between 500 and 550 people in pursuit of leads, the investigative team faced significant challenges. They compared a composite sketch of a potential suspect with 15 individuals connected to the case, yet none matched, leading to their exclusion as suspects. Only a handful of these men had any conceivable reason to be aggrieved with Andrew or Patricia, making them unlikely candidates in the traditional sense of suspects.

Detective Sgt. Joseph Zimmerman reflected on the process, acknowledging that many individuals involved were merely in the wrong place at the right time. Middlesex County Prosecutor Richard S. Rebeck quantified the effort: about 4,000 man-hours and $100,000 spent by personnel from his office, local police, and the federal Bureau of Alcohol, Tobacco, and Firearms.

By May 1982, the intensity of the bombing investigation had substantially diminished. Detectives were reassigned to the case on a part-time basis, a significant reduction from the initial 14 county, federal, and local law enforcement officers who were assigned full-time at the outset.

However, by the first anniversary of the incident, the investigation had hit a dead end. Various leads were followed, but none were fruitful. These included searching the home of a neighbor based on enough evidence for a search warrant, but nothing of significance was found. An anonymous tip suggested Andrew Puskas had a hostile letter exchange with an atheist in a publication, but a thorough examination of newspapers yielded no relevant information. Investigators delved into Andrew Puskas' military background to check if he had bomb training, only to find his role was primarily as a supply clerk, making this theory unlikely. There was a brief consideration that Andrew might have planted the bomb himself to target Patricia, planning to be safely away with their children at the time of the explosion. However, this theory was quickly discarded due to the absence of any marital problems.

In a more unconventional approach, an ATF employee consulted Rev. Kay Horman, a Virginia-based psychic, who claimed to receive visions and words about two men being involved in the bombing. Despite her detailed descriptions, her information did not lead to any significant breakthrough.

Friends of the Puskas family speculated that the murders might be connected to their strong religious beliefs. Rebeck suggested that their religious dedication could have antagonized someone, hinting at personal hatred as a potential motive.

At the time of the Puskas bombing, residential areas emerged as prime targets for bombing incidents, including those perpetrated by terrorists. The average suburban police officer was ill-equipped and lacked the specialized training required to safely handle explosive devices.

In a sobering revelation, a 1980 FBI report on domestic bombings underscored a concerning trend. It indicated that towns with populations of 10,000 or fewer, a common demographic in Central New Jersey, experienced a disturbing 25 percent surge in bombing attacks compared to the previous year. The report also shed light on a striking fact: while criminal bombings had historically been attributed to terrorists, a significant shift had occurred. More frequently, such acts of violence were carried out by disgruntled individuals seeking vengeance against their personal adversaries.

The Bureau of Alcohol, Tobacco, Firearms, and Explosives (ATF) identified two primary motives behind the planting of bombs: vandalism and vengeance. In the chilling case of the Puskas bombing, investigators held a strong belief that revenge had been the driving force behind the devastating tragedy.

The aftermath of the explosion that claimed the lives of Andrew and Patricia Puskas in 1982 was marked by formidable challenges. Despite relentless efforts, no arrests were made, and the case gradually faded into obscurity by the mid-1990s, leaving it unsolved to this day.

During the course of their investigation, authorities briefly explored the possibility of Ted Kaczynski, the infamous Unabomber, as a suspect. However, they found no substantial connection to the crime.

To provide support for the Puskas children, two trust funds were established, amassing donations exceeding $38,000. One of these funds was managed by the Puskas' church, while the other, known as the Puskas Children's Fund, was set up by the Police Benevolent Association Local 181.

Following the devastating loss of their parents, the Puskas children were entrusted to the care of an aunt. However, her struggles to manage all three children led to a difficult decision, resulting in the two older boys entering foster care, while the youngest, Brian, remained with her.

By 1992, the brothers were reunited and had settled into an undisclosed location in New Jersey.

The heart-wrenching saga continued with the passing of Jeannette Puskas, Andrew's mother. She suffered a massive heart attack while visiting the graves of her son and daughter-in-law, ultimately succumbing on June 4, 1982.

A year after the tragic event, the lot at 182 First Street, once the cherished home of the Puskas family, lay barren. It held only a few trees, a "for-sale" sign, and a swing set that had been thoughtfully crafted by Andrew Puskas for his beloved children. In time, the lot was sold, and a new home was constructed in its place.

Recognizing his extraordinary bravery, Officer Robert Schwarz, who had heroically extinguished the flames that engulfed Andrew Jr. and Scott Puskas, was honored with an award for valor by the Middlesex Borough Council.

On the solemn occasion of the first anniversary of the explosion, neighbors united in a touching gesture. They illuminated their porch lights to pay heartfelt tribute to the memories of Andrew and Patricia.

The Adelaide Disappearances

In the picturesque landscape of Adelaide in 1966, the Beaumont family carved out a seemingly idyllic existence. Jim Beaumont, the patriarch, held the profession of a linen goods salesman, a role that had him traversing the localities to liaise with clients, ensuring their linen needs were meticulously met. His life was complementarily balanced by his wife, Nancy Beaumont, a dedicated housewife whose days were filled with nurturing and caring for their three cherished children.

Their journey as a family began with the birth of their first child, Jane, in the breezy month of September 1956. The Beaumonts' joy doubled with the arrival of Arnna in the cool embrace of November 1958. Finally, their trio of joy was completed with the birth of Grant, their only son, in the warm month of July 1961.

Nestled in the suburbs of Somerton, their abode at 109 Harding Street stood as a symbol of small-scale, picture-perfect domestic bliss. For those familiar with historical mysteries, the name "Somerton" might ring a bell as the site where the enigmatic and unidentified Tamam Shud case unfolded in 1948. However, that intriguing mystery remains a separate tale, shrouded in its own enigmatic aura.

Life for the Beaumonts seemed like a dream come true. A stone's throw away from the serene beach, their home was ensconced in a suburb renowned for its tranquil beauty and understated elegance. By all accounts, the family of five was flourishing, basking in the joys of suburban life and the close-knit community around them.

Yet, unbeknownst to them, the winds of fate were starting to shift, foreshadowing a dramatic and distressing change in their lives. What lay ahead was a turn of events so unexpected and profound that it would etch their story into the annals of history, a tale of hope, mystery, and the unpredictable nature of life itself.

In the lead-up to their heartrending vanishing, the Beaumont children had started to show signs of growing independence. Jim and Nancy Beaumont placed their trust in their eldest, nine-year-old Jane, to look after her younger siblings, Arnna and Grant, during their frequent beach excursions. A short bus ride was all it took for them to reach their sandy haven.

The Beaumonts, residing in their tranquil Adelaide suburb, felt a comforting sense of security. The thought of any danger lurking in their community seemed unfathomable. They lived in a world where the safety and wellbeing of their children seemed assured, free from the anxieties that might plague a less serene setting.

As the Australian summer blazed on, with temperatures soaring beyond 40 degrees Celsius, Jim and Nancy saw no reason to hinder their children's beach visits. These outings had become a regular, uneventful part of life, with the children returning home safely time after time.

Despite their inherent shyness, these beach trips were beneficial for the children, offering them a chance to interact with others outside the confines of school and to stay active under the sun. Arnna, the spirited seven-year-old, even teased about Jane having a beach boyfriend, a comment the family took lightly, seeing it as nothing more than a child's playful jest.

On January 25th, in a twist of fate, Jim accompanied his kids to the beach before departing on a business trip, unknowingly bidding them farewell for an extended period. Grant, at four years old, reassured his father with innocent confidence, "Don't worry, Daddy. We'll be fine."

The morning of January 26th, 1966, dawned as any other. It was Australia Day, a festive occasion akin to America's Fourth of July or Canada Day, marked by a celebration of Australian heritage and pride.

With the day heating up, Nancy casually agreed to her children's request to visit the beach, a decision made easier by her plans to meet a friend. She handed them eight shillings and sixpence for beachside snacks and watched them head to their usual bus stop, just a block away at the corner of Harding and Diagonal Road.

Witnesses, including the bus driver, noted the children boarding the bus around 10:10 AM. One particular observer remembered Jane holding her favorite book, "Little Women," and could even recall the distinctive colors of the children's clothing, lending credibility to her account.

By 10:15 AM, the bus was en route to Glenelg Beach—a name intriguingly palindromic, as noted in a "Thinking Sideways" podcast episode about the case.

However, the next hour or so in the Beaumont children's timeline is shrouded in uncertainty. The local postman, familiar with the kids, reported seeing them walking towards the beach on Jetty Road. His initial account placed this sighting in the morning, although he later contemplated it could have been in the afternoon, introducing a slight ambiguity to the timeline.

Around 11:00 AM, an elderly woman near the Holdfast Sailing Club observed the children playing in a sprinkler at Colley Reserve, a common area for kids to frolic.

Finally at the beach, an hour after their arrival, numerous bystanders remembered seeing the children, but the bustling Adelaide tourist scene made it hard to keep track of everyone. The same elderly woman who saw them earlier also noticed a young man in blue swim trunks, initially lying face-down in the grass, but later actively engaging with the children.

Based on observations from the elderly woman and corroborated by at least three other witnesses, the mysterious man observed with the Beaumont children was described as being around six feet one inch tall, with a lean build, blond hair, and a thin face. His attire consisted of a blue bathing suit, and he seemed to have been observing the children for some time before engaging with them.

This unidentified individual, estimated to be in his early-to-mid-thirties, has since become a focal point of suspicion in the case. Various theories have surfaced over the years regarding his identity and possible motives.

One lingering speculation suggests that this man might have been the "boyfriend" Arnna alluded to, although this connection remains unverified. Notably, the children were seen leaving the beach with this unknown man, further intensifying the mystery surrounding their disappearance.

The sighting of the children with the man, while concerning, was not their last known interaction. Subsequently, they were observed at Wenzel's cake shop, sometime between 11:45 AM and 12:15 PM. The exact timing of their visit is subject to varying accounts.

At the shop, the children purchased pastries, and notably, a meat pie, using a one-pound note. This detail raises several questions. Firstly, it was uncharacteristic for the children, particularly before lunch, to opt for a savory item like a meat pie over sweets, as remembered by their parents.

Secondly, the source of the one-pound note is puzzling. Nancy Beaumont distinctly remembered giving her children only eight shillings and sixpence, insufficient for such purchases. This discrepancy suggests that the children might have received additional funds from an external source, presumably the unidentified man from the beach.

The whereabouts of this man during the children's visit to the cake shop remain unknown. It's conceivable that, if his intentions were malevolent, he would have preferred to avoid being seen with the children. He could have been waiting outside or nearby, perhaps on a bench, anticipating their return.

Further accounts from witnesses suggest that the Beaumont children interacted with the unidentified man in ways that raised alarm. He was seen assisting the children in dressing after they had played in the sprinklers at Colley Reserve, a behavior that struck onlookers as unusual. Observers presumed he must be a relative, given the children's comfortable demeanor around him.

However, this contradicts known details about the children, particularly Jane. Nancy Beaumont later reflected that her daughter was quite shy, making it unlikely for her to feel at ease with a stranger helping her dress. Although Jane was a spirited young girl, she was not naive to the point of blindly trusting a recent acquaintance.

An incident involving an older lady and a pair of grandparents with their granddaughter further adds to the mystery. They reported being approached by the man, who inquired about someone tampering with his clothes and mentioned missing money. Following this, he began dressing the children, taking his time in a manner that appeared unsettling to the witnesses.

Tragically, this would be the last confirmed sighting of the Beaumont children.

Nancy Beaumont, expecting the children to return home on the noon bus, was surprised when they didn't disembark at their usual stop, just a block from their home. She assumed they might have missed the bus and would either walk home or catch the next one, a decision not unusual for the time and place.

In the hours following their last confirmed sighting, there were two more potential but unverified sightings. The first involves Tom Patterson, the local postman, who initially claimed to have seen the children in the morning. He later altered his statement, suggesting a possible afternoon sighting that would align with them missing the noon bus. However, his route timing makes this uncertain.

The second sighting was reported by a tourist from Broken Hill. He claimed to have seen three children, resembling the Beaumonts, with a man matching the description of the unknown individual, but with lighter brown hair. This discrepancy led to doubts about the accuracy of this sighting.

As the hours passed, Nancy Beaumont waited anxiously at home. The two o'clock bus came and went without any sign of Jane, Arnna, and Grant.

Jim Beaumont, engaged in linen sales with a business partner in Snowtown, two hours north, returned home around three in the afternoon. He was met with the distressing news that their children, Jane, Arnna, and Grant, had not been seen for hours. Nancy had been anxiously awaiting any news or sighting of them at their home.

The couple immediately embarked on a frantic search, retracing the possible routes their children might have taken to and from the beach. Their efforts, spanning several hours, yielded no results; no sign of their children or any of their belongings, including their towels, clothes, or Jane's beloved "Little Women" book, was found.

By 7:30 that evening, with the children missing for nearly ten hours, Jim and Nancy contacted the police. Jim continued the search through the night, while

Nancy stayed home in hope of their return.

The next morning, the Beaumont children were officially declared missing, and the police initiated a full-scale investigation. They began by piecing together the children's last known movements, informed by witness accounts from the beach area. This helped establish a timeline of events.

Early on, the possibility of the children being swept away by the tide was dismissed. The absence of any personal items on the beach suggested a different scenario. Had they been taken by the sea, it was likely that at least one belonging would have been left behind.

The case swiftly captured national attention in Australia. Five days later, on January 31st, Jim and Nancy made a heartfelt appeal on TV and radio, pleading for their children's safe return.

The police were inundated with hundreds of tips, each meticulously investigated, but all leading to dead ends. Reports of children seen alone or with a man flooded in, sparking numerous searches but failing to yield any concrete leads.

Every individual linked to the Beaumonts, including neighbors, family friends, and Jim's coworkers, came under scrutiny. Adelaide was abuzz with efforts to find any trace of the children, with particular attention on the blonde man seen with them. He was quickly identified as a prime suspect, and sketches based on eyewitness descriptions were circulated.

About two weeks following the disappearance of the children, a local newspaper received a mysterious phone call. The telephonist who answered described the caller as having a distinct "foreign accent." Before she could transfer the call to the newspaper's chief of staff, the man on the line claimed to have the Beaumont children and demanded a substantial reward for their return. However, the call was abruptly ended before it could be transferred, and the police, though not dismissing it outright as a hoax, have not disclosed whether this lead was pursued further.

This incident was one of several where the investigation was potentially clouded by pranksters and false leads. From the outset, the investigation faced immense challenges. Extensive searches of nearby beaches, caves, and coves yielded no clues or belongings of the missing children.

Months later, the case saw a glimmer of hope when a woman came forward with a crucial testimony. Six months after the children's disappearance, she reported witnessing a man leading two girls and a boy into an abandoned house next door on the night the Beaumonts vanished. She claimed to have seen the boy leave the house later, only to be chased and captured by the man.

The woman's delayed report, coming six months after the event, raises questions about its credibility and her motives for withholding such vital information. The frustration surrounding this delay is palpable, as it could have been a significant lead had it been reported promptly.

In the ensuing months, the flow of useful information dwindled. Despite ongoing reports of suspects and sightings, the case remained unsolved. The disappearance of the Beaumont children not only heightened vigilance among parents but also became a cautionary tale that would resonate for decades.

In November 1966, Gerard Croiset, a 57-year-old Dutchman who identified himself as a parapsychologist and psychometrist, entered the saga of the Beaumont children's disappearance. Croiset, whose methods were rooted in spirituality and paranormal beliefs rather than scientific evidence, had previously gained some recognition in Europe for his involvement in criminal cases, including aiding Dutch police after World War II.

His arrival in Australia, at the invitation of wealthy businessman Con Polites, reignited media interest in the case. However, this attention was not entirely positive, as it veered the investigation into the realm of spectacle. Jim and Nancy Beaumont, along with the police, were skeptical of Croiset, dismissing him as a charlatan. Nonetheless, the public, driven by hope and desperation, clung to the possibility that he might uncover a crucial lead.

Upon visiting Glenelg Beach, where the children were last seen, Croiset made a bold assertion. He claimed that the children had not been abducted but were instead trapped under the floor of a newly constructed warehouse. He confidently stated that he would locate the children within two days, professing, "I have had a vision of where the children started from. I will walk there and a vision will come to me immediately. I am 90 percent sure I will pinpoint the place where the bodies will be found."

Despite police skepticism, public support led to the raising of over $40,000 to excavate the warehouse floor. However, the search yielded no evidence of the Beaumont children, nor any indication they had ever been there.

Croiset's visit to Australia ended without success. Years later, in 1996, when the warehouse was scheduled for demolition, it was again excavated by Con Polites, who had financed Croiset's trip. Yet, this effort too failed to uncover any trace of the missing children.

In 1968, a letter, allegedly penned by eleven-year-old Jane Beaumont, arrived at the Beaumont residence. Postmarked from Dandenong, a suburb of Melbourne, it was the first of two letters believed to be written by Jane, a conclusion drawn by the police after comparing the handwriting to Jane's old school assignments.

The letter conveyed that Jane, Arnna, and Grant were in the care of an unidentified individual referred to as "the Man." According to the letter, "the Man" was taking good care of them, ensuring their safety and well-being. Soon after, another letter was delivered, this time supposedly authored by "the Man" himself. He claimed to have assumed guardianship of the children but expressed a willingness to return them under certain conditions.

Jane's letter included specific instructions for their father, Jim Beaumont: to wear a dark coat and white pants for identification and to avoid informing the police. The letter expressed eagerness for a reunion but stressed the importance of secrecy from the authorities.

Driven by a glimmer of hope, Jim Beaumont traveled over 700 kilometers to Dandenong, Victoria, and waited near the post office for three days. Despite the Beaumonts' initial reluctance, they informed the police, who discreetly monitored the area. The situation attracted media attention, resulting in a bustling crowd outside the post office.

Unfortunately, the wait was in vain. No one came forward with the children, and Jim returned home empty-handed. Following this, a third letter arrived, also purportedly from Jane, stating that "the Man" had been present in Dandenong but fled upon spotting an undercover officer. The letter accused the Beaumonts of betrayal and indicated that "the Man" would retain custody of the children.

Twenty-five years after the Beaumont children's disappearance, advancements in forensic science enabled detectives to conduct DNA testing on the letters previously believed to have been written by Jane and "the Man." This testing revealed a startling truth: the letters were penned by a 41-year-old man who was a teenager at the time of the incident. His actions, intended as a cruel prank, had added a layer of false hope and deepened the anguish of the Beaumont family.

By the time of this discovery, the statute of limitations for filing charges against the individual had expired. The man, now remorseful for his actions as a teenager, expressed regret for contributing to the Beaumont family's prolonged suffering. However, his belated guilt pales in comparison to the relentless torment and unanswered questions that haunted the Beaumonts for decades.

On a bustling Saturday afternoon, the Adelaide Oval, a prominent stadium in northern Adelaide, was alive with the fervor of a football match. Among the fifty-thousand spectators, two families, familiar with each other through their regular attendance as season ticket holders, sat side by side, united by their shared passion for the sport.

In their midst were two young girls: eleven-year-old Joanne Ratcliffe, a regular at the weekend matches with her parents, and four-year-old Kirste Gordon, who, despite her tender age and limited grasp of the game, accompanied her grandmother to the event.

During the match, Joanne needed to use the restroom. Given permission by her parents, she was also entrusted with accompanying Kirste, as requested by Kirste's grandmother. The girls returned from their restroom visit without incident, and the game continued amidst the deafening cheers of the crowd.

However, about half an hour later, Kirste needed to visit the restroom again. Joanne, displaying a nurturing instinct beyond her years, volunteered to escort Kirste once more. They set off towards the restroom around 3:45 PM.

As minutes ticked by without the girls' return, concern began to ripple through their families. This concern soon escalated into panic. While the match proceeded, Joanne's parents embarked on a frantic search towards the restrooms, leaving Kirste's grandmother at their seats in case the girls came back.

Twenty minutes after their departure, Joanne's mother reached the secretary's office, requesting a PA announcement. Her request was declined, with the explanation that the noise of the crowd would drown out the announcement. Mrs. Ratcliffe later speculated that the staff was reluctant to disrupt the ongoing match.

For the next hour, the Ratcliffe family scoured the Adelaide Oval, searching desperately for Joanne and Kirste. Their efforts led to a stadium announcement being made approximately an hour later, following Mr. Ratcliffe's appeal to the secretary of the South Australian cricket association.

By 5:12 PM, the situation had escalated to a full-scale emergency, with the girls reported missing to the local police. The subsequent police search mirrored the Ratcliffe's in its lack of results, marking the beginning of another distressing chapter in the community's history.

The immediate aftermath of the disappearance of Joanne Ratcliffe and Kirste Gordon was deeply unsettling. The police gathered witness accounts that painted a troubling picture, with multiple sightings of a man accompanying the two girls under distressing circumstances. What was particularly alarming was the similarity between this man's description and that of the individual seen with the Beaumont children seven years earlier at Glenelg Beach. He was described as tall and gaunt, with sketches from both incidents bearing resemblances to each other.

Several witnesses recounted seeing the man carrying Kirste, with Joanne visibly resisting and protesting. This led authorities to theorize that the man had seized an opportunity to abduct Kirste, and Joanne had instinctively followed, attempting to intervene. In one instance, the man, burdened by Kirste, told Joanne to leave, but she persisted, pleading for them to be allowed to return to their families.

The girls were spotted up to three kilometers away from the Adelaide Oval, with the last sighting occurring around ninety minutes after they went missing, coinciding with the onset of the police search.

Tragically, Joanne Ratcliffe and Kirste Gordon would never be seen again. Their disappearance, like that of the Beaumont children, left their families in a state of perpetual uncertainty and sorrow.

As years passed, the Beaumont case and the Adelaide Oval abduction remained unresolved, with no significant leads or credible witnesses coming forward. The Beaumont children, if still alive, would have grown into teenagers or adults, but there was no indication that they remembered or could return to their previous lives.

Jim and Nancy Beaumont continued to reside at their Harding Street home, clinging to the hope that their children might one day return. Nancy even preserved a muddy palm print on a sliding glass door, a poignant reminder of her son. Eventually, the strain took its toll, leading to their divorce and withdrawal from public life.

The Ratcliffe and Gordon families similarly faced the heart-wrenching task of moving forward without closure. The hope of their daughters' safe return gradually dimmed as months turned into years.

Both cases remained stagnant until 1979, when the community of Adelaide would confront further heartache. The unresolved mysteries of the past were not the end of the city's tragedies, but rather a prelude to more sorrow yet to be uncovered.

In the shadows of 1979, the tranquil setting of South Para Reservoir in Northeast Adelaide was shattered by a grim discovery: the body of a 17-year-old young man. This event unfurled the beginning of a harrowing chapter in Adelaide's history, known as the Family Murders. A tale so shrouded in darkness and enigma, it seems to leap straight from the pages of a crime thriller.

These Family Murders, spanning from 1979 to 1983, claimed at least five young lives, all teen boys and young men. Each tragic discovery revealed a tale of unimaginable horror: the victims had been subjected to severe torture and mutilation, enduring sexual abuse of the most heinous nature before their untimely deaths. The brutality of these acts suggested a chilling precision, hinting at the disturbing possibility of an organized ring behind these abductions and killings.

Diving into the details of these crimes is a daunting task, even for a seasoned true crime enthusiast like myself. The sheer savagery inflicted upon these young men evokes a visceral reaction, a mix of horror and profound sadness.

As the investigation unfolded and the victims' stories came to light, a suspect emerged from the shadows. The case turned a corner in 1983 when drugs were detected in the system of the fifth victim. This discovery led authorities to a man known as Bevan Spencer von Einem.

Labeling von Einem as merely "evil" seems an understatement. This roughly forty-year-old accountant was charged with the unthinkable: the kidnapping, torture, sexual assault, and murder of Richard Kelvin, a fifteen-year-old boy. As investigators peeled back the layers of von Einem's story, inconsistencies and lies began to surface. Claiming to have been alone at home, ill with flu on the night of Kelvin's disappearance, his alibi crumbled when evidence directly linked him to the crime. Fibers from his clothing and hairs, later confirmed as his, were found on Kelvin's body. Von Einem's explanations became increasingly convoluted, veering from denial to improbable excuses.

Ultimately, the weight of evidence against von Einem was overwhelming. He was convicted and sentenced to life imprisonment, with his no-parole period initially set at 24 years, later extended to an Australian record of 36 years. While he was only convicted for Kelvin's murder, many believed von Einem was involved in the other Family Murders. Yet, he never confessed to these crimes, and to this day, despite the evidence, maintains his innocence.

The Family Murders gradually receded from public attention. However, speculation about the existence of a larger criminal organization, of which von Einem was supposedly a part, persisted. The theory was that this group went into hiding following von Einem's conviction but may have been behind numerous other disappearances in the Adelaide area.

Post-conviction, theories about von Einem's potential involvement in other high-profile cases, such as the disappearance of the Beaumont children, emerged. These speculations were fueled by the testimony of "Mr. B," a former associate of von Einem and a member of Adelaide's gay community. Mr. B claimed that von Einem had admitted to the murders of the Beaumonts and two girls at the Adelaide Oval, leading to a fallout in their friendship. This testimony, albeit sensational, lacked concrete evidence and was tainted by Mr. B's history of drug use and criminal behavior. Thus, any connections drawn between von Einem and these cases remain speculative and largely unsupported.

As for von Einem's potential link to the Beaumont children, the evidence is tenuous. The suspect seen with the children on the day they vanished was described as being in his mid-thirties, while von Einem was only about twenty at the time. Furthermore, physical discrepancies, such as von Einem's dark-ish brown hair, contrasted sharply with the blonde hair described by witnesses.

Today, Bevan Spencer von Einem continues to serve his life sentence, a pariah in Australian society for his role in the vile Family Murders. His story serves as a stark reminder of the depths of human depravity. In 2007, South Australia's Premier Mike Rann vowed to enact legislation ensuring von Einem would never walk free again. His infamy, stemming from these heinous acts, endures, marking him as one of Australia's most despised figures. Despite his conviction, the full extent of his crimes and the true story behind the Family Murders remain shrouded in mystery.

In 1998, a "Crimestoppers" TV segment revisited a haunting cold case from 1970 in Townsville, a coastal town in northeastern Queensland, Australia. The case involved the tragic murder of two young sisters, five-year-old Susan and seven-year-old Judith MacKay. On the morning of August 26th, 1970, they were last seen waiting at their school bus stop.

Two days after their disappearance, a shocking discovery was made in a dry creek bed: the bodies of the MacKay sisters, with their school uniforms meticulously folded in their bags beside them. The girls had been brutally raped, stabbed, and strangled. For nearly three decades, their murders remained an unsolved mystery in a region far removed from the notorious Beaumont and Adelaide Oval disappearances.

The MacKay family endured years of agonizing uncertainty until the 1998 "Crimestoppers" episode aired. Following the broadcast, the show's phone line received a crucial tip from a caller who believed she recognized the suspect's description. She identified him as her cousin's husband, a man she knew all too well from her own harrowing experiences as a victim of his molestation and other illegal activities.

Arthur Stanley Brown, then 86, had been a lifelong resident of Townsville. As investigators delved into his background, they uncovered a horrifying past. In the months that followed, detectives gathered evidence leading to over 45 charges against Brown. These included molestation, sexual assault, pedophilia, and the murders of Susan and Judith MacKay. Crucial to building their case were the testimonies from Brown's own family members, including those from his wife's family, many of whom had suffered molestation or sexual assault at his hands, some even taken to the very creek bed where the MacKay girls were found.

Investigators discovered that Brown, around sixty at the time of the murders, had been employed as a carpenter at the girls' school. His behavior following the murders raised serious red flags. Most bizarrely, he removed and buried the door of his car – a vehicle matching descriptions provided by eyewitnesses of the abduction. Brown's justification for this odd act was to avoid harassment, given the similarity of his car to the one used in the crime. He later exhumed and disposed of the door in a junkyard. Adding to the suspicious behavior, Brown had an unsettling fixation with the murder case and even took two young relatives to the crime scene.

But Brown's disturbing actions extended beyond the MacKay case. Allegations surfaced of numerous victims spanning decades, from his younger years to old age. Additionally, the mysterious circumstances surrounding the death of his first wife, Hester, in 1978, raised further questions. Hester's death certificate was issued without a proper examination, and her body was quickly cremated.

Following Hester's death, her younger sister Charlotte, along with her five children, moved in with Brown. Brown and Charlotte married just months later, seemingly unfazed by the recent tragedy.

In 1982, another one of Hester's sisters accused Brown of molesting her, leading to revelations of similar experiences from several family members. Despite this, legal counsel advised against court action to avoid potential trauma for the victims, leaving these horrific acts as buried family secrets until they were unearthed by the "Crimestoppers" episode in 1998.

In 1999, the curtain was finally drawn back on the long-hidden deeds of Arthur Stanley Brown, as he was brought to trial in his 80s. Having evaded justice for most of his life, Brown seemed on the brink of outmaneuvering the law one final time. Despite compelling evidence and testimonies, including confessions he allegedly made decades earlier, Brown eluded conviction due to his deteriorating mental health.

The trial in 2000 faced setbacks due to issues with circumstantial evidence, leading to delays. In a twist, media reports emerged stating that the trial could not proceed for undisclosed legal reasons. It was later revealed in 2001 that Brown's advancing dementia and Alzheimer's disease rendered him unfit for trial, leaving him unable to stand or plead in court.

Brown might have avoided legal justice, but his life took a bleak turn. In 2002, his wife Charlotte passed away, and he found himself ostracized by his family. His funeral was a quiet, almost secretive affair, attended by only one stepdaughter. Weeks later, a stepson bitterly commented on Brown's profound, yet destructive impact on so many lives.

For the MacKay family, there was a sense of closure in knowing that Brown was responsible for the rape and murder of Judith and Susan. Following his death, police officially closed the case file, convinced of his sole culpability.

However, Brown's death also reignited speculation about his possible involvement in other notorious cases, including the Beaumont children's disappearance and the Adelaide Oval abduction. Despite being based in Queensland, far from Adelaide, an investigation into his holiday records yielded no results, leaving open the possibility that he could have traveled undetected. His tendency to hide evidence, like the buried car door, only fueled these suspicions.

A witness from his trial recalled Brown mentioning a visit to the Adelaide Festival Centre during its construction, placing him in Adelaide around the time of the Adelaide Oval abduction. Adding to the intrigue, Brown physically resembled the sketches of the suspects from both the Beaumont and Adelaide Oval cases. However, his age at the time made it unlikely for him to be mistaken for a younger man.

One detail stood out: during the Adelaide Oval abduction, a witness noted the suspect wore horn-rimmed glasses, which fell off during his escape. These glasses were a staple of Brown's appearance, even in his younger years.

While there's a possibility that Brown was involved in these other disappearances, conclusive evidence remains elusive. His death in 2002 meant any remaining secrets died with him.

In the years since, other suspects have emerged in these cold cases. Figures like James Ryan O'Neill and Derek Earnest Percy have been mentioned in connection with the Beaumont case, though these links are often weak. Another suspect, Arthur Stanley Hart, who died in 1999, gained attention for the Adelaide Oval abduction following the discovery of a secret basement on his property.

In 2013, "The Satin Man" was published, suggesting wealthy Adelaide businessman Harry Phipps as the Beaumont children's abductor. This theory, based on family testimonies, was not pursued further by the police.

As the fiftieth anniversary of the Beaumont children's disappearance passed, the mystery continues. Their parents, now in their nineties, live privately, perhaps still hoping for answers. Just before the anniversary, a new tip rekindled interest in the case. With a substantial reward still on offer, authorities acknowledge that any breakthrough would likely come from a deathbed confession or inside information.

The Adelaide authorities urge anyone with knowledge to come forward. Meanwhile, the fates of Jane, Arnna, and Grant Beaumont, along with Joanne Ratcliffe and Kirste Gordon, remain one of Australia's most enduring mysteries.

Murder of Denise Davenport

Greeley, a vibrant city in Colorado, is nestled 30 miles southeast of Fort Collins and roughly 50 miles northeast of the bustling city of Denver. This town, serving as the county seat of Weld County, is also the proud host of the University of Northern Colorado, a hub of academic and cultural activities.

Named after the influential American editor Horace Greeley of the _New-York Tribune_, Greeley has a rich history intertwined with the Colorado Gold Rush, originally known as Pike's Peak Gold Rush, which began in 1859. Horace Greeley, a notable figure of his time, is often remembered for his impactful slogan, "Go west, young man, and grow up with the country," encouraging the youth of America to explore and grow with the expanding frontiers.

In the heart of Greeley, Denise Davenport was born in August 1964, to Hal and Carrie Davenport. She grew up with her sister, Debbie, in a family that saw its share of changes, including their parents' divorce. Following the separation, Hal remarried and settled in Grand Junction with his new wife, Anita, while Carrie moved to Littleton.

Denise, a striking figure with her petite frame and sandy blond hair, was not just an average student. By her junior year, she was deeply involved in the academic and social life at the University of Northern Colorado. As a dedicated member of a UNC sorority, she balanced her educational pursuits with the lively activities of sorority life.

Her life in Greeley was not confined to the university campus, though. Denise also engaged with the broader community, working part-time at the Greeley Mall. This job allowed her to connect with the town's vibrant atmosphere and its people, adding another dimension to her college experience.

Denise Davenport's life in Greeley, Colorado, was a blend of academic pursuits and social engagement. Her boyfriend, Doug Kandel, 25 years old, often spoke of her as "really friendly, outgoing, and easily approachable," a personality that made her well-liked among her peers. Despite her outgoing nature, Denise was cautious, especially when it came to being alone. She valued the safety in numbers, often joining her friends for walks to the James A. Michener Library on the university campus, embracing both the camaraderie and the security it provided.

On February 24, 1985, a day etched in the memory of her loved ones, 20-year-old Denise left her job at the mall around 5:15 pm. She had plans, not just ordinary plans, but significant ones. She had borrowed Doug's sports car and intended to visit the car wash, a mundane errand before a momentous evening. Denise was scheduled to be inducted as an officer in her sorority that night, a recognition of her leadership and commitment.

However, the evening took an unexpected and worrying turn. Denise never made it to the induction ceremony. Her absence raised immediate concerns among her friends, especially when she uncharacteristically missed classes the next morning. The community of Greeley, usually calm and serene, was now clouded with worry and uncertainty.

The following day, February 25, a disturbing discovery was made. Doug's car was found abandoned on the university campus near Frazier Hall. The details were unsettling: the doors were unlocked, the radio still playing, and the driver's seat was pushed back. Doug was convinced that someone else had driven his car, as Denise was always meticulous about locking the car and turning off the radio.

Adding to the mystery, police discovered dirt on the driver's seat and the undercarriage of the car. However, this clue led nowhere; the soil was consistent with that found throughout the Greeley area, offering no unique insights into Denise's whereabouts.

In a twist, a witness reported seeing a car at an intersection on the night of Denise's disappearance, its hazard lights flashing ominously. She also noticed a young woman, potentially Denise, walking with two men towards a pawn shop. This sighting sparked a new direction in the investigation, but despite the efforts of the authorities, this lead, too, reached a dead end.

The disappearance of Denise Davenport sent shockwaves through her family, drawing them together in a desperate search for answers. Hal Davenport, an electrical contractor, and his wife, Anita, felt the impact deeply and wasted no time in traveling to Greeley upon hearing of their daughter's disappearance. Denise's mother, Carrie, driven by a mother's concern, made the journey from Littleton, uniting with her former husband and his family in a common cause that transcended past differences.

In an effort to coordinate the growing search efforts, Denise's boyfriend, Doug Kandel, opened his home to serve as a command center. It became a hub of activity, with volunteers streaming in, some from as far as Cheyenne, Wyoming, all united by a single goal: to find Denise. The community's response was a heartening display of solidarity and compassion, with people from all walks of life coming together to support the Davenport family in their time of need.

A massive search operation unfolded, spearheaded by law enforcement officials and bolstered by the tireless efforts of volunteers. In a remarkable display of determination and community spirit, they produced and distributed 7,000 posters and 5,000 handbills, spreading the word far and wide, even reaching out to Grand Junction, where Hal and Anita lived.

For two long months, the search continued, a period marked by hope, despair, and relentless determination. Then, on a fateful Saturday, April 20, 1985, the grim reality surfaced. Two kayakers on the South Platte River made a harrowing discovery: the nude body of a young woman, floating between 18th Street and Highway 34. The Weld County Coroner, Paul Stoddard, identified the body through dental records as Denise Davenport. The state of decomposition was severe, obscuring the cause of death, leaving more questions than answers.

Stoddard later declared that Denise's death was "not a natural death." The lack of evidence of a stabbing, gunshot wound, or drug overdose only deepened the mystery. He eventually listed "homicidal violence of an undetermined type" on the death certificate, a phrase that encapsulated the baffling and tragic nature of the case.

The investigation into Denise Davenport's murder was fraught with challenges. The detectives faced a daunting task with little physical evidence to guide them. The next logical step was to draw comparisons between Denise's case and other unsolved murders in and around Weld County, in hopes of finding a pattern or connection that could lead to a breakthrough.

In a haunting parallel, Vicki Carpenter, a 25-year-old woman, also fell victim to an unsolved murder. Her disappearance occurred in the shadowy hours between February 18 and 19, 1985, just days before Denise vanished. Vicki's body was discovered in the Cherry Creek spillway on April 2, 1985, in a macabre state, weighed down with concrete. Her last known whereabouts were at a bar and restaurant in East Denver.

The similarities between the two cases were striking and unnerving. Both victims were young, attractive women of similar ages and appearances. Their disappearances occurred within a close timeframe, and tragically, both were found dead in bodies of water in April 1985. The advanced decomposition of their bodies rendered the causes of their deaths undeterminable, adding a layer of complexity and frustration to the investigations.

Despite these eerie parallels, the authorities were unable to establish a definitive link between the murders of Denise Davenport and Vicki Carpenter. Vicki's case, like Denise's, remained a dark, unresolved mystery.

The investigation into Denise's past revealed a brush with the law in 1983. The _Greeley Tribune_ reported that she was arrested for the sale of hallucinogenic mushrooms and was implicated in a UNC drug investigation, which also involved her boyfriend, Doug Kandel. Denise had cooperated with the police, leading to a plea of guilty to misdemeanor possession. She received a suspended six-month jail sentence and a fine, a situation that might have created tensions in her personal relationships.

Doug Kandel, who knew Denise's whereabouts on the night she vanished and had loaned her his car, was briefly considered a suspect. Investigators speculated whether resentment over Denise's cooperation with the police in the drug case might have played a role. However, no evidence surfaced to implicate him in her murder.

The drug angle was also explored as a potential motive for Denise's murder, but this line of inquiry led nowhere.

In a development that reignited public interest, Weld County Sheriff Harold Andrews announced a significant lead at a press conference on April 26, 1985. The investigation concluded that Denise's body had likely been thrown into the South Platte River on the night she disappeared. Witnesses reported seeing a four-wheel-drive vehicle near the two bridges area on the night of February 24. The vehicle was said to have become stuck, leading to speculation that the driver either sought help or hitchhiked from the scene.

Sheriff Andrews, maintaining a cautious approach, refrained from divulging further details to protect the integrity of the ongoing investigation.

Mid-May 1985 saw authorities intensifying their search efforts in the vicinity of the South Platte River. Reporter Luke Clarke detailed the meticulous nature of the investigation, noting that "Six cubic yards of earth were taken from a point on the river near where the body was found. Screens normally used in archaeological digs were used to sift through dirt." (_The Daily Sentinel_, May 15, 1985). This methodical approach underscored the gravity of the situation and the determination of the investigators to leave no stone unturned.

During this painstaking search, authorities discovered clothing items near the river. Intriguingly, these clothes did not match Denise's size, adding another layer of mystery to the already complex case. However, the police maintained a strict code of silence regarding any additional findings, fueling speculation and anticipation in a community already on edge.

In a dramatic twist, Larimer County Sheriff Jim Black called a press conference to announce a potential breakthrough. He linked Denise Davenport's tragic death to Larry Eugene Blehm, a 41-year-old man with a criminal record. Blehm, who ran a plant store across from the car wash Denise intended to visit on the night of her disappearance, had already attracted the attention of law enforcement.

Blehm's arrest on March 15, 1985, for suspected involvement in a series of burglaries in the Red Feathers area, had Larimer County deputies collaborating with the Weld County Sheriff's Office. Additionally, Blehm was being investigated in connection with three homicides in Larimer County – those of Allen Sorenson, 79, his wife, Doris, 69, and Donald Ova, 32, of Greeley.

Despite Sheriff Black's announcement, Weld County Sheriff Harold Andrews expressed reservations, deeming the connection "premature." He revealed that Blehm was merely one of three suspects under consideration and cautioned against labeling him the prime suspect in Denise's case. The identities of the other two suspects remained undisclosed, deepening the intrigue surrounding the investigation.

In a turn of events, Larry Blehm was never charged in connection with any of the murders, including Denise's. Sheriff Black stood alone among law enforcement officials in naming Blehm as a suspect in her death.

Years later, in February 2009, the _Greeley Tribune_ was approached by Jerome Santiago, then 33 years old, who brought forward a startling claim. He suspected that his mother's former boyfriend, Max, could be responsible for Denise's murder. However, the newspaper refrained from publishing Max's surname, as he had never been officially named as a suspect by the police.

The mystery was further complicated by an intriguing testimony from Jerome, who was just nine years old in 1985. He grew up in a tumultuous household south of La Salle, where his mother's heavy drinking and the parade of different men she brought home created a chaotic environment.

In a revealing interview with _Greeley Tribune_ reporter Mike Peters, Jerome recounted a disturbing incident from early 1985. He vividly remembered a man named Max, emerging from a cornfield, appearing drugged and deranged, leading to one of the most intense altercations between Max and his mother. During their heated exchanges in the days following Denise's killing, Jerome overheard the name "Denise Davenport" being mentioned multiple times.

This potential lead, as reported by the _Tribune_, was to be passed on to Weld County sheriff's detective Vicki Harbert. However, the outcome of this tip, whether it was pursued or led to any significant findings, remained shrouded in mystery, leaving another loose thread in an already complex tapestry of the case.

The narrative took another unexpected turn in late November 2011. Former Arapahoe County Sheriff Patrick Sullivan, then 68, was embroiled in controversy, accused of exchanging methamphetamine for sex with a male acquaintance. Sullivan, who served as sheriff from 1984 to 2002, had a surprising connection to Denise: she had been his babysitter before attending UNC. Hal Davenport, Denise's father, recalled Sullivan's selectiveness in choosing babysitters for his children, mirroring the Davenports' own cautious approach.

Hal Davenport held Sullivan in high esteem, particularly for his assistance during the search for Denise. Sullivan had facilitated connections with the police and the district attorney, providing the Davenport family with crucial information and support. Despite this close association, neither Hal nor Denise's mother, Carrie, who passed away in 2004, ever suspected Sullivan of being involved in their daughter's death.

Sullivan's name was also linked to another tragic case - that of Sean Moss, 27. After retiring as sheriff, Sullivan became a security chief at Cherry Creek School district and hired Sean, who was found dead in the South Platte River near Denver in January 2011. Intriguingly, Sullivan had bailed Sean out of jail shortly before his murder. Toxicology reports indicated the presence of a date rape drug and methamphetamine in Moss' system.

The connection between the locations where Denise and Sean's bodies were found – both in the South Platte River – could not be ignored. However, the state of decomposition of Denise's body made it impossible to determine if drugs were in her system.

Sullivan's interest in Denise's case was evident when he visited the Weld County Centennial Center to inquire about her death, expressing his personal connection to Denise. Yet, the police never considered him a suspect in her murder. Sullivan later served time in Arkansas Valley Correctional in Ordway, CO, and was released in 2015.

As the 35th anniversary of Denise Davenport's murder approached, Detective Byron Kastilahn from the Weld County Sheriff's Office announced a renewed investigation into her case, along with several other unsolved crimes involving women. Detective Kastilahn, who joined the department in 2019, brought over two decades of law enforcement experience to these cold cases, offering a glimmer of hope that justice might yet be served.

Murder of Tamla Horsford

Tamla Horsford, aged 41, was an embodiment of love and joy, known for her radiant smile and heartwarming presence. Born in the picturesque St. Vincent and the Grenadines in 1978, she embarked on a life-changing journey to the United States with her family in 1989, a move that would shape her future in profound ways.

In the sunny climes of Florida, Tamla's life took a romantic turn when she met Leander Horsford. Their love blossomed, leading to a union where Tamla embraced Leander's daughter from a previous relationship as her own. Together, they welcomed five sons, creating a bustling, loving household. The family later relocated to Georgia, driven by Leander's career opportunities.

2018 was a year of anticipation and joy for Tamla and Leander, as they were on the cusp of becoming grandparents. Their excitement was palpable, but fate had a different plan, and Tamla would tragically never meet her grandchild.

Tamla's zest for life was undeniable. She was often described as the "life of the party," a testament to her vivacious and spirited nature. In November of that year, she was invited to a birthday and slumber party at the home of her friend, Jeanne Meyers. Their friendship had blossomed through their sons' school sports activities.

The party, organized by Meyers' friend Stacy Smith, was intended to be a relaxed, enjoyable gathering, with an emphasis on safety as attendees planned to stay overnight to avoid driving under the influence.

On November 3, 2018, Tamla lovingly prepared a breakfast casserole for her family before setting off to the party. Although she arrived later than the 7 p.m. invitation time, her entrance at Meyers' residence on Woodlet Court around 8:30 p.m. was marked by her characteristic warmth. She brought a bottle of Tequila as a birthday gift for Meyers, and donned unique white onesie pajamas adorned with paw prints, standing out as the only black woman at the gathering.

The party, a BYOB affair, was initially planned as a women-only event. However, the presence of Meyers' boyfriend, Jose Barrera, and Smith's husband, Tom Smith, added an unexpected dynamic. The Smiths had hosted a gender reveal party earlier that day, and with their home still bustling with guests, Tom preferred to stay at the party with Stacy.

The gathering at the Meyers' residence on that fateful night comprised a group of twelve individuals, later referred to as the "Forsyth 12" by those advocating for Tamla. This group consisted of nine women, including Jeanne Myers, Madeline Lombardi, Stacy Smith, Nichole Lawson, Marcy Hardin, Paula Seals, Bridget Fuller, Sarah Cockerham, and Jennifer Morrell. Accompanying them were two men, Jose Barrera and Tom Smith, as well as Jennifer's husband, who was responsible for dropping off and picking up his wife.

The evening's agenda was a blend of casual socializing, enjoying a variety of foods, sipping on alcoholic beverages, and engaging with the Alabama–LSU football game. The women congregated on the main level of the home to watch the game and chat, while the men opted to view the game in the comfort of the finished basement.

Tamla, known for her smoking habits, frequently took breaks to smoke cigarettes on the balcony. She was also observed smoking marijuana once during the evening, but was requested by Meyers to refrain from continuing due to Barrera's occupation as a pretrial officer.

The party dynamics shifted as the men joined the women during the halftime of the football game, leading to a group activity of playing Cards Against Humanity. In a moment of familial connection, Tamla took the opportunity to FaceTime with her children during the game.

Throughout the evening, the group captured memories in the form of pictures and videos. Notably, in these visuals, Tamla did not exhibit any signs of distress or excessive intoxication; rather, she seemed to be thoroughly enjoying herself.

Despite the initial plan for all guests to spend the night, a few decided to leave the party early. Sarah Cockerham, Bridget Fuller, Marcy Hardin, and Nichole Lawson chose not to stay overnight.

The party gradually wound down, with guests beginning to retire to bed around 1:30 a.m. Tamla, however, remained awake. Bridget Fuller was reportedly the last person to interact with Tamla. Around 1:45 a.m., Fuller encountered Tamla in the kitchen, enjoying a bowl of gumbo. Tamla mentioned her intention to smoke a cigarette before heading to bed. Shortly thereafter, at 1:47 a.m., Fuller left the party, escorted by her husband, Gary Fuller.

Intriguingly, Nile Cappello of Rolling Stone documented that within a span of ten minutes, from 1:47 a.m. to 1:57 a.m., the home's security system recorded the back door being opened, closed, and then finally left open at 1:57 a.m. Additionally, the system logged the garage door's activity, noting it opened and closed at 1:30 a.m. and again at 1:40 a.m., though the reasons for these occurrences remained unexplained.

The following morning at about 8:30 a.m., Madeline Lombardi, Jeanne Meyers' aunt living in the basement of the Meyers' home, woke up and went downstairs to make coffee. She noticed something unusual in the backyard - it was Tamla Horsford, identifiable in her unique paw-print onesie, lying face down. Taking a moment for a quick prayer, Lombardi then went upstairs to alert Meyers and Barrera about the situation.

Lombardi initially hesitated to knock on Meyers' door, thinking she overheard the sound of running water, so she waited briefly before knocking again. Upon their response, she urgently informed them about Tamla's state, referring to her as Meyers' "friend from the islands."

Shortly before 9 a.m., Meyers placed a call to 911. In the conversation with the dispatcher, both Meyers and Barrera provided details about Tamla's condition. Meyers suggested that Tamla might have fallen off the balcony due to her drinking, while Barrera noted Tamla's immobility and lack of breathing, describing her as being stiff.

Police officers from Cumming arrived at the scene within 15 minutes, followed by paramedics. However, Officer Corey Moore decided not to engage the paramedics' services, and neither Barrera, who had CPR training, nor the police officers attempted to resuscitate Tamla.

Two hours after their arrival, Tamla was declared dead at the scene. Barrera later mentioned to the police about finding a cigarette and lighter on the upper deck, which led investigators to hypothesize that Tamla might have stepped out for a smoke around 1:57 a.m. and accidentally fell, causing her death.

The investigation concluded that Tamla's death was an accident, with no evidence of foul play. Leander Horsford, Tamla's husband, recalled being told by the authorities that Tamla may have tripped over garden edging, leading to her fatal injury, a similar accident that Lombardi had previously experienced and survived.

However, several aspects of the investigation were concerning. The police did not collect fingerprints or other potential evidence, and the medical examiner did not conduct a thorough investigation, omitting the use of a sexual assault kit and not collecting fingernail scrapings. Moreover, despite Meyers having security cameras at her house, they were not recording on the night of Tamla's death.

The medical report on Tamla Horsford's death, completed by Associate Medical Examiner Andrew Koopmeiners, concluded that her injuries were consistent with those sustained in a fall. However, the extent and nature of Tamla's injuries raised questions. She had experienced severe trauma including blunt force injuries to her head, neck, torso, and extremities, a broken neck, a dislocated wrist, and a laceration to her right ventricle, along with various abrasions and cuts.

The position in which Tamla was found also seemed unusual for a fall. She was face down with her legs extended and feet pointing to one side, and one arm was bent at the elbow. Interestingly, her facial injuries were minor, despite the severe trauma to other parts of her body.

The toxicology report indicated a high Blood Alcohol Content (BAC) of .238, suggesting significant impairment. Despite this, party attendees did not perceive her as intoxicated, and she wasn't seen holding a drink in group photos, unlike some others. Additionally, THC and Alprazolam (an anxiety medication) were found in her system, though friends stated she did not take Alprazolam.

Authorities did not test Tamla for illegal drugs, citing a policy of not testing for such substances when the potential suspect is deceased. This decision was met with criticism, especially considering the use of the term "suspect" in this context.

Ralph Fernandez, the lawyer representing Tamla's family, after reviewing the evidence, suggested that homicide could be a strong possibility. He pointed out that some of Tamla's injuries, particularly scratches on her hands, appeared to be defensive wounds, indicating a possible struggle or attack.

Fernandez also noted a significant omission in the investigation – the lack of autopsy photos, which he found unusual and suspicious, suggesting they might have been intentionally not taken. Despite the Forsyth County Sheriff's Office (FCSO) and the Georgia Bureau of Investigation (GBI) claiming that autopsy photos were taken and maintaining that Tamla's death was accidental, Fernandez expressed doubt, especially since the GBI mentioned the need for a release from Tamla's next of kin only after public questioning.

Detective Mike Christian's handling of the investigation was criticized for his delayed response in interviewing the party attendees, which began several days after the incident and continued over a two-week period. This delay in gathering first-hand accounts was seen as a significant flaw in the investigative process.

During the investigation, interviews were conducted with Jeanne Meyers, Jose Barrera, and Madeline Lombardi at Meyers' home on November 9, rather than at the Forsyth County Sheriff's Office. Other interviews with party attendees took place on subsequent dates throughout November.

Detective Mike Christian's approach to these interviews was notably passive. He typically began by asking interviewees to describe the party and events in a general manner, allowing them to lead the narrative. His responses during the interviews were minimal, often limited to simple affirmations like "Mm-hmm" or "Ok," and he seldom interjected with questions of his own.

When Christian did pose questions, they frequently focused on Tamla's consumption of alcohol, her smoking habits, and whether she used marijuana. This narrow line of questioning, centered heavily on Tamla's behavior and choices, drew criticism for its apparent fixation on her use of substances.

Christian's questioning also included seemingly irrelevant or odd inquiries. For instance, he asked Barrera about the type of food served at the party, a detail that seemed trivial in the context of the investigation. Another peculiar question was directed at Lombardi regarding whether she had adjusted her clock for daylight saving time, which appeared to have little bearing on the case.

At the end of each interview, Christian consistently asked a broad, open-ended question, inquiring if there was anything he might have missed or should have asked. This approach was seen as indicative of a lack of thoroughness or direction in his investigation.

The investigation was further criticized for Christian's manner of questioning, which sometimes came across as leading and disinterested.

Jeanne Meyers, in particular, stands out in the group for her actions during the investigation. During an interview with Lombardi, Meyers offered Dunkin Donuts gift cards to the investigators, Detective Christian and his colleague Tyler Sexton. Although the detectives declined the gift cards, this gesture by Meyers could be perceived as an attempt to curry favor.

Moreover, Meyers' social media activity added an element of controversy to her involvement. A post on her Facebook page in December 2020, accompanied by a suggestive hashtag, seemed to allude to insider knowledge or a shared secret among the group. This, coupled with a picture showing her with friends, all sporting similar hairstyles, added to the intrigue and suspicion surrounding her role in the events.

There are also inconsistencies in Meyers' own account of the party. She claimed to have arrived at her party around 7:15 p.m. and mentioned that Tamla was the last to arrive at 8:30 p.m. However, this contradicts the statements of Paula Seals and Nichole Lawson, who indicated that Seals was the last to arrive, closer to 10 p.m.

In Meyers' interview, when asked whether Tamla had made it to bed that night, Meyers initially stated that Tamla never made it to the bed, then quickly clarified that the bed was never messed up, suggesting a hasty correction in her narrative.

Adding to the ambiguity, Meyers made a Facebook status update the day after the party, contradicting the investigators' findings about Tamla's fall from her deck. This post was later deleted, but not before it was captured in a screenshot by CBS46. Despite her lawyer's attempts to explain it away, this post by Meyers raised further questions about her version of events and her understanding of what happened that night.

The inconsistencies in the statements made by those present at the party where Tamla Horsford was last seen alive add to the confusion surrounding the events of that night.

Madeline Lombardi, for instance, reported waking up around 8:30 a.m. on November 4th and discovering Tamla's body after making coffee in the basement. Jennifer Morrell, another party attendee, mentioned waking up between 7:30 and 7:45 a.m. and preparing to leave by 8 a.m. She observed Lombardi acting unusually in the kitchen around this time. Later, Morrell adjusted her timeline to align more closely with Lombardi's account, which raises questions about the accuracy of her statement.

Lombardi also noted in her statement that Tom and Stacy Smith left the party in the early morning, but the couple themselves stated they left after 8 a.m. There are conflicting accounts about when the guests arrived; some said between 7 and 7:30 p.m., while Lombardi claimed Nichole Lawson arrived at 4 p.m., contradicting Lawson's statement of arriving at 6 p.m. Additionally, Lombardi's account puts Jeanne Meyers and Stacy Smith arriving much earlier than Meyers' own claim of arriving at her house at 7:15 p.m.

There were also discrepancies about the timing of events at the party.

Lombardi claimed to have been on the balcony with Tamla before the game started around 8 p.m., but others mentioned Tamla arriving at the party between 8 and 9 p.m. The group photo, which Lombardi said she took before the game started, did not include Paula Seals, who hadn't arrived yet, although Meyers and others claimed the photo was taken at halftime.

As for Bridget Fuller, Lombardi stated that Fuller and her husband arrived before 7 p.m., but Fuller did not mention her husband being at the party, and Jennifer Morrell stated her husband only dropped her off. Fuller's own statement included her bringing blueberry vodka for the nine women at the party, a specific count excluding Tamla, which was odd considering there were ten women, including Tamla, at the party.

Fuller also wore sleep pants in the group photo but claimed she didn't stay overnight, explaining she didn't like sleeping in other people's beds. She also mentioned Jose Barrera being cropped out of the group photo, though he and others said he spent the first half of the game downstairs.

The accounts given by the guests at the party where Tamla Horsford was last seen vary significantly, adding to the confusion surrounding the events of that night. Contrary to some claims that Tamla was the last to arrive, it was actually Paula Seals who arrived last. Sarah Cockerham initially didn't recall seeing Tamla go out to smoke, despite others saying she did, later remarking that she wasn't paying attention.

Jennifer Morrell's statement about Tamla arriving in her pajamas contradicts others who said Tamla changed into them at the Meyers' house. There was a curious consistency in the way the guests described Tamla's Tequila bottle, almost as if they had coordinated their responses, yet Lombardi mentioned Tamla drinking Vodka instead.

The familiarity of the guests with Tamla was also inconsistent. Some claimed they did not know her well or had just met her that night, which seems unlikely given their mutual connection with Jeanne Meyers, known to be sociable.

The incident report and the police interviews present conflicting information about Tamla's level of intoxication. While the report suggests she was heavily intoxicated, the guests' statements during police interviews indicated that she did not appear overly intoxicated and there was uncertainty about the amount she drank.

The use of crime scene tape by the police, particularly in the living room, raises questions given that Tamla's death was classified as an "accidental fall." Tyler Sexton's observation that Tamla's pajamas were clean, without any grass or debris, seems inconsistent with a fall outdoors.

Detective Mike Christian's note about marks on Tamla's shins possibly corresponding with landscaping metal found near her feet is not corroborated by crime scene photos. Additionally, discrepancies exist in the timeline of events, with Meyers stating that guests went to bed at 1:30 a.m., while the report suggests 1 a.m., and Bridget Fuller reported seeing Tamla eating gumbo in the kitchen at 1:45 a.m.

Lombardi's account of discovering Tamla's body also differs between her interview and the incident report. She told Christian she saw the body through a basement window, but the report indicates she went outside to check the weather and then found Tamla.

An intriguing aspect is the mention of Michael J. Pallerino, aged 55, in the police report, an individual not previously noted in other accounts or interviews, adding another layer of mystery to the already complex case.

By February 2019, the group of individuals involved in the party where Tamla Horsford was last seen, known as the "Forsyth 12," had secured legal representation and complained about receiving threats from Tamla's supporters.

Michelle Graves, a close friend of Tamla and a vocal advocate, firmly believed that Tamla was killed by someone at the party and her body was thrown over the balcony. In response to this, seven members of the Forsyth 12 filed a lawsuit against Graves for her accusatory social media posts in February 2019, which was later dismissed by a judge. However, the group appealed, and for reasons unexplained, Jeanne Meyers and Jose Barrera were no longer part of the lawsuit.

Tamla's family, along with many of her supporters, did not accept the explanation that her death was accidental. Supporters of the department, on the other hand, reportedly harassed those who criticized the Forsyth County Sheriff's Office (FCSO) in connection with Tamla's case.

Ashland Harris, who campaigned for reopening Tamla's case and started a Change.org petition, faced her own challenges. She was detained by a Cumming police officer in November 2019 during a search for individuals involved in a car accident. Despite being cleared, she filed a complaint against the officer, which was dismissed by Police Chief David Marsh. Harris later faced further trouble when FCSO deputies arrived at her home with a warrant for her electronic devices, accusing her of sending accusatory emails to one of the party attendees. Harris denied this and filed a lawsuit for civil rights violations against Detective Jeffrey Roe and Sheriff Ron Freeman.

Detective Mike Christian, who was involved in the investigation, was rumored to have a complicated personal life, including extramarital affairs. One of his girlfriends claimed that Christian had shared pictures of Tamla's body and confidential case details with her. Another woman corroborated this, stating that Christian freely shared sensitive information about the case.

An internal investigation found that Christian had indeed been sending case-related pictures and information to women he was involved with. He resigned in January following these revelations. In a statement, Christian expressed regret over his actions and the impact on his career, stating his commitment to his marriage and acknowledging the consequences of his choices.

This series of events and revelations adds further complexity and controversy to the already troubled investigation into Tamla Horsford's death, casting a shadow on the conduct of those involved in the case.

Murder of Morgan Jade Violi

organ Jade Violi's life began on a crisp autumn day, November 3, 1988, in the rolling hills of Kentucky. Born to Glen and Stacey Violi, Morgan entered a family rich in love and complexity. Her world was shared with two older half-sisters, Heather Prewitt Coleman and Nikki Prewitt Britt, who had lost their biological father. Glen, embracing fatherhood with open arms, raised Heather and Nikki as his own, weaving a tapestry of unity and affection in their lives.

The year 1993 marked a turning point for the Violi family. Glen and Stacey's paths diverged, leading to their separation. Despite the familial shift, Morgan, a beacon of joy and intelligence, continued to thrive. She lived at the Colony Apartments complex off Shive Lane, a bustling hub of community life, with her mother and sisters. Stacey, always effusive in her praise, described Morgan as a "beautiful, friendly, smart" child, who wore her heartwarming smile like a crown.

July 24, 1996, dawned like any other summer day, with the sun casting a warm glow over Kentucky. The air was filled with the scent of freshly cut grass, and the skies were a brilliant shade of blue. It was the perfect backdrop for a day of childhood adventures. Seven-year-old Morgan, brimming with the boundless energy of youth, and her friend set off for the playground within their apartment complex. Heather and Nikki were nearby, keeping a watchful eye on their younger sister. Heather, with a sister's instinct, reminded Morgan to put on her shoes, a small act that spoke volumes of their closeness.

The clock struck 12:36 p.m., a moment that would forever be etched in the Violi family's memory. As Morgan and her friend navigated the parking lot, heading back to their apartment, an unforeseen horror unfolded. A man, driving a burgundy or red Chevrolet van, emerged with nefarious intent. He initially grabbed Morgan's friend but quickly shifted his focus to Morgan, throwing her into his van.

Heather, alerted by Morgan's screams, rushed towards the scene, only to be met with a chilling sight: a man sitting in the van, smiling sinisterly at her. In a fleeting moment, she saw Morgan's friend darting between the apartment buildings. Initially, Heather thought it was a playful chase, but the grim reality soon dawned on her as she realized Morgan had been abducted. Eyewitnesses, including the friend and an adult, promptly alerted the authorities.

The Bowling Police Department, in tandem with the FBI, launched a massive search and investigation operation. The community was on high alert, with tips flooding in at a rate of one every 10 to 15 minutes. By Friday, July 26, the authorities had mobilized teams, each comprising a city police officer and an FBI agent, to investigate over 100 tips. The urgency of the situation was such that the police postponed more than 200 felony investigations to dedicate their full attention to Morgan's kidnapping.

The Bowling Green Police, in a fervent bid to rescue the little girl, embarked on a meticulous search. Local motels were scrutinized, and hundreds of vans, mirroring the description of the abductor's vehicle, were stopped and checked. Despite these exhaustive efforts, the trail remained cold, leaving authorities and the community grasping for any shred of hope.

Amidst this turmoil, the community's spirit shone brightly. Nearly 400 individuals, united by a common cause, gathered for a candlelight vigil. This sea of flickering lights became a symbol of collective hope and solidarity, as prayers and positive thoughts were sent out for Morgan's safe return.

In an attempt to hasten the search, the FBI released a composite sketch of the suspected abductor. However, the situation was complicated by varying witness descriptions. Some described the suspect as a 6-foot tall white male with a beard and collar-length brown hair, while others recalled short blond hair or curly brown hair. The suspect was dressed in a white T-shirt and blue jeans and was believed to be in his 20s or middle-aged. His vehicle, a key piece of evidence, was described as a burgundy or red van, possibly adorned with gold trim and bearing a Kentucky license plate.

Meanwhile, in Fairview Park, Ohio, near Cleveland, an intriguing lead emerged. Dawn Kurth, a waitress at an Applebee's restaurant, noticed a couple dining with a little girl who bore a striking resemblance to Morgan. The man accompanying the child bore a vague resemblance to the man in the FBI's sketch, while the woman with them was heavily made-up and wore a wig, adding to the air of suspicion.

Kurth, driven by a mix of intuition and concern, approached the child. She inquired about the little girl's name and her grade at school. The girl, who said she was seven and in the third grade, matched Morgan's age and school grade. When Kurth pressed further about the school she attended, the woman swiftly intervened, diverting the conversation.

Another employee at the restaurant overheard the woman referring to the girl as "Morgan," intensifying Kurth's conviction that the child was indeed Morgan Violi. Fueled by a sense of duty, Kurth promptly alerted several law enforcement agencies, including the FBI office in Louisville, hoping her observation could be the key to solving the case.

However, the investigation took a somber turn on Monday, October 21, 1996. In a heart-wrenching news conference, the police announced the discovery of the remains of a young girl, aged between 6 and 11, in Tennessee. The FBI suspected these remains to be those of Morgan Violi. The discovery was made by a woman walking on her property between Springfield and White House, who stumbled upon the remains near an old barn. Springfield, located about 15 miles from the Kentucky-Tennessee border and 40 miles from Bowling Green, suddenly became a focal point in this tragic story.

The investigation took a significant yet somber turn when authorities discovered remains that bore haunting similarities to the young girl. Among the remains, they found dark brown hair and a yellow barrette, items chillingly consistent with Morgan's last known appearance. She had been wearing a white shirt adorned with rainbow stripes, white shorts, pink "jelly" shoes, and notably, a yellow barrette in her hair. The scene, however, yielded no further clues, deepening the mystery surrounding the circumstances of her disappearance.

An autopsy was promptly conducted, and the findings were as grim as they were conclusive: the manner of death was determined to be a homicide. Despite this crucial finding, the police maintained a veil of secrecy over the finer details of the case, perhaps to protect the integrity of their ongoing investigation.

The investigative team faced a significant challenge in positively identifying the remains. The hair found at the scene was consistent with Morgan's, a critical lead, but the advanced state of decomposition coupled with the absence of Morgan's dental records hindered definitive identification.

In an innovative approach, University of Tennessee Professor Murray Marks, a respected forensic pathologist, collaborated with a Knoxville digital photography company. They embarked on a meticulous process, involving the scanning of Morgan's picture and converting video footage of Morgan's skull into separate computer files. This cutting-edge technique allowed for a detailed comparison.

Marks employed a meticulous method, using the teeth as guide marks. He carefully rotated the skull image, aligning it until the head's tilt matched the angle in Morgan's picture. This painstaking process was aimed at ensuring that if the teeth alignment was a match, a dentist could then make the final, irrefutable identification.

Within a day or two, the FBI delivered a heartrending announcement: the remains were conclusively identified as belonging to Morgan Violi. Marks, reflecting on the accuracy of the identification, remarked, "The teeth were a perfect match. They fit like a glove," a statement that brought a somber closure to one part of the mystery.

In a poignant backdrop to this tragic discovery, the details of Morgan's parents' divorce proceedings surfaced. On the morning of Morgan's abduction, a divorce hearing was scheduled for 10:30 a.m. Stacey Violi and Glen Violi had previously agreed that Stacey would be the custodial parent. However, in a twist of fate, Glen Violi was conspicuously absent from the court that day. The judge, proceeding with the hearing, awarded Stacey custody of Morgan and her sisters, while Glen was granted custody every other weekend. Glen later claimed ignorance of the hearing, stating he had gone to work, a claim supported by his lawyer who mentioned that Glen's presence was unnecessary due to a prior settlement of the custody arrangement.

The unraveling of Morgan Violi's abduction case took a complex and emotionally charged turn as the spotlight turned towards her father, Glen Violi. Glen, a hardworking man, embarked on a fateful workday on July 24, 1996. He commenced his laborious duties around 6:30 a.m., leading a six-man construction crew. Their task for the day was at an old farmhouse situated in Franklin, a location just shy of the Tennessee state line, approximately 19 miles to the south of Bowling Green.

As the morning sun rose higher in the sky, the crew toiled diligently, but around 11 a.m., they decided to break for lunch. Glen, in a seemingly routine sequence of events, dropped off his colleagues, tended to some errands, and made a stop at the Brass Box bridal store to get fitted for a tuxedo for an upcoming friend's wedding. Amidst the bustling day, he even bought his wife some flowers, a gesture of hope and optimism for the future of their relationship. In his own words from 1997, Glen reflected, "I thought we were really getting somewhere. I thought our marriage was working."

The clock neared 12:50 p.m., and Glen headed to the apartment where his wife and daughters resided, carrying with him the flowers he had lovingly chosen. Little did he know that this visit would forever alter the course of their lives. It was during this visit that he received the agonizing news of Morgan's abduction, a moment seared into his memory.

Glen's talents extended beyond his construction work; he was also an accomplished artist. Fueled by a father's desperate desire to help find his daughter, he took it upon himself to sketch a composite image of the abductor based on witness descriptions. However, the sketch drew mixed reactions, with some individuals noting a resemblance to Glen himself, a twist that added layers of complexity to the investigation.

In his pursuit of truth and justice, Glen found himself under the intense scrutiny of law enforcement. He recounted undergoing several polygraph tests at the hands of the FBI, each one yielding a distressing outcome - failure. However, throughout this ordeal, Glen unwaveringly maintained his innocence regarding his daughter's abduction and subsequent tragic fate. According to him, the FBI harbored suspicions that he may have been involved in hiring someone to harm his own flesh and blood, a theory that further strained an already fraught situation.

Morgan's mother, Stacey, initially shared Glen's disbelief in his potential involvement in their daughter's abduction. However, as the grim reality of Morgan's fate came to light with the discovery of her remains, their communication dwindled, and Stacey made the painful decision to keep Glen from seeing their other daughters, Heather and Nikki. The familial bonds that once held them together strained under the weight of grief and suspicion.

Over time, though, Stacey's perspective evolved, and she came to no longer believe that Glen played any part in Morgan's tragic end.

The investigation into Glen Violi's possible involvement spanned two years, ultimately culminating near the second anniversary of Morgan's abduction in July 1998. As the media reported, articles from 1996 and 1998 portrayed Glen as never having been officially named a suspect. However, newer reports began to paint a different picture, muddying the waters of an already complex and heart-wrenching case.

The tireless pursuit of justice for Morgan Violi involved the dedicated efforts of FBI Special Agent Dick Glenn, who was assigned to her case in 1996. His unwavering commitment to unraveling the mysteries surrounding Morgan's abduction and murder would span many years.

In a candid interview with WBKO in 2016, Agent Glenn shed light on a critical breakthrough in the case. He revealed that the van used in Morgan's abduction had been stolen from a residence in Dayton, Ohio, just a day prior to the tragic event. Subsequently, the van was abandoned at a truck stop in Franklin, Tennessee, in close proximity to where the horrifying abduction had taken place. Remarkably, law enforcement managed to recover the stolen 1978 van a mere three days after the abduction occurred. However, the crucial forensic link that would tie the van definitively to the abduction wouldn't be established until March of the following year, further underscoring the complexity and painstaking nature of the investigation. The van was found at the Union 76 truck stop, serving as a tangible but enigmatic piece of evidence in the case.

Adding to the intrigue, the Robertson County Sheriff's Office website provided intriguing details about a second vehicle possibly linked to the case. This vehicle, described as a "1979 or older white Ford Van with a slatted trailer-door type window on the side," was observed parked near an old barn on North Swift Road at Webster Road in Robertson County on July 25th, 1996, just a day after Morgan's abduction. Strikingly, this location was a mere 100 feet from where the remains of Morgan Violi would be tragically discovered on October 20th, 1996. However, the barn that once stood witness to this grim event had since vanished, leaving only memories and questions in its wake.

Despite the relentless efforts of law enforcement and the community, the case of Morgan Violi remained shrouded in darkness. No one has ever been arrested or held accountable in connection with her abduction and murder, a stark reminder of the elusive nature of justice in some cases.

Disappearance of Misty Copsey

Born under the shadow of her parents' separation in 1978, Misty Copsey's life unfolded like a vibrant tapestry, rich with challenges and triumphs. Diana Smith and Buck Copsey, her parents, parted ways shortly after her birth, leaving young Misty to find solace and strength in her mother Diana's care.

As a beacon of academic excellence and athletic prowess, Misty shone brightly in her school. Her days were filled with the thrill of sports - softball, basketball, and volleyball - and she juggled these with a consistent B-average, a testament to her dedication and balance.

Misty's magnetic charisma and a quirky sense of humor were keys to her popularity. Her friendships were deep and meaningful, especially with Trina Bevard, affectionately nicknamed "Bean" by Misty, who in turn was dubbed "Bunyan". Their bond was unique, woven together by shared secrets and the kind of laughter that only best friends understand.

In the halls of her junior high school, Misty was more than just a popular girl; she was a cherished friend, admired for her genuine warmth and friendliness.

Her early years were spent in the humble surroundings of Green Meadows mobile park in Puyallup, a place where she forged lasting friendships. In 1992, Diana, striving for a better life for them, moved to a duplex in Spanaway, a short distance but a whole new world for Misty. This change brought new challenges, but Misty's resilient spirit shone through.

Diana's job as a caregiver often kept her away at night, leaving Misty to her own devices. Yet, she maintained close ties with her Green Meadows friends, ensuring the bonds of friendship remained unbroken despite the distance.

Among these friends was Rheuban Schmidt, an older boy from the trailer park with a complex and unreciprocated interest in Misty. He was drawn to her, a feeling not shared by Misty, who saw him more as a means to mobility with his green 1974 Chevy Nova than a romantic interest. This dynamic caused tension, particularly with Diana, who was protective of her daughter.

Misty, beginning to explore the world of crushes and attraction, had her sights set on a different type of boy - the athletic, charming types epitomized by celebrities like Jason Priestley. Rheuban, unfortunately for him, didn't fit this ideal in Misty's eyes.

Misty's journey through these formative years was a mosaic of experiences - from navigating her parents' divorce to finding her place in a new neighbor- hood, from cherishing deep friendships to confronting the complexities of young relationships. Her story is a tapestry of resilience, youthful exuberance, and the bittersweet nuances of growing up.

The relationship between Misty and Diana Copsey echoed the typical ups and downs of a mother and teenage daughter. Diana, while grappling with her own challenges with alcohol, managed to maintain a stable life for herself and Misty.

One summer, a mix-up led to a tense moment when Diana, unable to find Misty, filed a missing persons report. The confusion was soon resolved when Misty was found safe at home, but the incident remained a filed case, perhaps a reflection of the pre-cell phone era's communication challenges.

Speculation about Diana's struggle with alcohol playing a role in this mix-up lingers, but it remains just that - speculation.

In the months leading up to Misty's disappearance, their relationship appeared to be thriving. Diana's gifts of a new stereo and clothes to Misty not only brought joy but also seemed to strengthen their bond, providing Misty with both material comfort and personal freedom.

As Misty embarked on a new school year at Spanaway Lake Junior High, the excitement of the approaching Puyallup Fair was in the air. She and her best friend Trina looked forward to a day of fun at the fair, unaware of the impending tragedy.

Meanwhile, Cory Bober, driven by a relentless conviction, was convinced that Randy Achziger was the infamous Green River Killer. His suspicions were fueled by a crucial clue allegedly overheard by Achziger from an inebriated Auburn police captain. Bober's pursuit to prove Achziger's guilt became a crusade, involving the media and intense scrutiny from local authorities.

Bober's efforts initially led Pierce County and King County detectives to consider Achziger as a suspect. However, after thorough investigation, they removed him from their list of suspects, much to Bober's frustration.

Undeterred, Bober intensified his efforts, resorting to unconventional methods and even threatening vigilante justice. His fixation on Achziger strained his relationships with law enforcement, particularly with Puyallup Police Sergeant Herm Carver, who, along with others, grew weary of Bober's persistent interference.

In 1992, Bober's attention turned to a pattern of killings in Puyallup. Despite his warnings to local detectives about an imminent murder, his credibility had been so diminished by his previous actions that his cautions were largely ignored.

In September 1992, Bober's ominous prediction hovered in the air, but without the attention it might have once commanded, as the community remained unaware of the tragedy that was about to unfold.

On September 17th, Misty Copsey finally got the green light from her mother, Diana, to attend the fair without adult supervision. She was set to go with her best friend, Trina, but needed to sort out her ride back home. Confident she could either take the bus or get a lift from a friend, Misty was content with the plan. To reassure Trina's parents, Diana agreed to a small deception, implying she would be providing transport for both girls to and from the fair.

Diana's commitment to her job as a caregiver for an elderly person meant she couldn't drive the girls herself, but she was willing to bend the truth a bit to be the "cool parent" for once. The understanding was that as long as Misty and Trina caught the right bus, everything would be fine.

For the fair, Misty chose a pair of her mother's fashionable, oversized stonewashed jeans, which she had to roll up to fit. The night promised to be exciting, especially with Huey Lewis and the News performing at the fairgrounds, drawing large crowds to Puyallup, a town that otherwise had a small-town feel.

With the weekend looming, Misty was thrilled to spend an evening with her best friend, savoring a newfound sense of independence.

The plan was to take the 8:40 PM bus home, connecting Misty from downtown Puyallup to Spanaway. This gave the girls a full day to immerse themselves in the fun of the fair.

However, they got so caught up in the excitement that they missed the crucial 8:40 bus, the last one for the night on that route. Now, Misty needed to find an alternative way back to Spanaway.

Trina, living in Sumner, had the option to walk home, as it was much closer to the fairgrounds. But for Misty, residing atop South Hill in Spanaway, walking wasn't feasible.

At 8:45 PM, Misty called her mother to inform her about missing the bus. Diana, understandably upset yet constrained by her caregiving responsibilities, advised Misty to seek a lift from a friend. When Misty suggested Rheuban, her older admirer, Diana firmly opposed the idea.

Diana suggested Misty use her new electronic organizer to find someone else for a ride and insisted she call back once she had secured one. Tragically, that return call never happened.

As the hours ticked by without a return call from Misty, Diana's worry escalated. She was stuck at work, caring for her elderly patient, with no choice but to hope Misty had safely found a ride home. Perhaps, even from Rheuban, though the thought was not comforting.

Returning home later, Diana was greeted by silence. The empty house, devoid of Misty's presence, amplified her anxiety. She started a frantic round of phone calls - reaching out to Trina, Rheuban, Misty's grandmother, and other friends. In the early morning, answers were scarce. Trina's family was unreachable, and her grandmother hadn't heard from Misty. Rheuban did respond, explaining that he couldn't help Misty due to a lack of gas.

As dawn broke, Diana's concern turned into panic. A call to 911 brought little relief; she was mistakenly informed she had to wait 30 days to report a missing person, labeling Misty as a potential runaway.

Determined, Diana drove to Trina's house, leaving a note urging a callback. By the afternoon, she managed to file a report with the Pierce County Sheriff's Department, learning that the "30 days" policy was incorrect. However, jurisdictional complications arose; since Misty vanished in Puyallup, Pierce

County couldn't act without Puyallup PD's approval, who still considered Misty a runaway.

Diana tirelessly retraced Misty's steps and reached out to anyone connected to her daughter. The day was a blur of panic and emerging heartache. Trina eventually called back, having seen Diana's note. She shared that they had separated the previous night as Misty headed to her bus stop, and she hadn't seen or heard from her since.

On a hunch, Diana called Rheuban's home again and spoke with his roommate, James Tinsley, who shockingly claimed Rheuban and his uncle had picked up Misty. This revelation fueled Diana's suspicions.

When she called back later, Rheuban was home and his story changed: he hadn't picked up Misty but had gone to a party with his uncle. The inconsistency in his account was troubling, but Diana's immediate concern was finding her daughter.

In the ensuing days, Diana clung to a fading hope. If the Puyallup police were right and Misty was a runaway, perhaps she would return or reach out. Diana didn't believe this but had to maintain some hope.

Diana Smith's world was upended in the wake of her daughter Misty's disappearance. From a hard-working mother cherishing her bond with her teenage daughter, she became a woman engulfed in a relentless search for Misty.

She tirelessly created and distributed fliers throughout the town, especially in the downtown area where Misty was last seen. Diana reached out to Misty's friends, imploring them to contact her if Misty appeared, assuring them there would be no consequences – her primary concern was Misty's safety.

In her relentless quest, Diana tracked down the bus driver who worked the

Spanaway route on the night Misty vanished. He remembered seeing Misty but had finished his shift for the night, advising her to catch a connecting bus from Tacoma to Spanaway.

As days passed, friends and family members, including Rheuban Schmidt, checked in, asking about any police progress. Diana, still harboring suspicions about Rheuban, felt the strain of time as hours turned into days.

Finally, on September 23rd, six days after Misty's disappearance, Diana managed to file a missing persons report with the Puyallup Police Department, which had jurisdiction over the case. She encountered a police force seemingly convinced that Misty was a runaway, expected to return or make contact soon.

Sergeant Herm Carver of the Puyallup Police, previously involved with Cory Bober, led the investigation. Initial efforts focused on the fairgrounds area, but soon shifted to scrutinizing Diana's background. They uncovered her past DUIs, a welfare fraud conviction, and a previous, unresolved missing persons report for Misty. These discoveries cast Diana in a dubious light for Carver, painting her as someone with a history of dishonesty.

On September 29th, Carver met with Diana at Misty's school, where they encountered two eighth graders spreading rumors of having seen or spoken to Misty since her disappearance. However, these students were mere acquaintances of Misty, not close friends. One claimed a phone call from a safe Misty in Olympia, and another alleged a sighting at a concert days after she went missing. Carver dismissed these claims as unreliable.

Leaving the school, Carver informed Diana that he was removing Misty from the missing persons database, categorizing her as a runaway. This decision was devastating for Diana, who firmly believed Misty was not a runaway but a contented and well-adjusted girl.

Years later, one of the students would confess to fabricating her statement for attention, casting further doubt on the investigation's direction.

The situation worsened when Carver spoke to a Seattle radio station, publicly declaring Misty a runaway and suggesting Diana knew of her whereabouts. This announcement effectively halted the investigation, leading to the removal of search fliers and a general cessation of efforts to find Misty.

In late September 1992, Cory Bober's pursuit in the Green River Killer case took a significant turn when he learned about Misty Copsey's disappearance from his mother. Receiving the missing person flier with Misty's picture was a pivotal moment for him, aligning with his long-standing investigation.

Bober reached out to Diana, eager to share his extensive theories about the Green River Killer, his prime suspect, and his frustrations with the police's apparent inaction. For Diana, Bober's involvement offered a glimmer of engagement in her daughter's case, beyond the official channels that seemed to have labeled Misty as a mere runaway.

However, Bober's theories also brought a grim perspective. He suggested that Misty had likely been abducted and killed by his suspect, shattering Diana's hopes of Misty's safe return. This revelation was devastating, confronting her with a harsh reality that clashed with the police's narrative.

United by a common goal, Bober and Diana became allies in seeking the truth about Misty's fate. They communicated frequently, with Bober often leading the discussions. This partnership provided Diana with a channel to process her grief, even as she struggled with alcohol.

Meanwhile, Bober, reinvigorated by this alliance, intensified his efforts. He contacted Sergeant Herm Carver of the Puyallup PD, who was already familiar with Bober's vendetta. Carver maintained that Misty was a runaway and informed Bober that the case had been transferred to the Pierce County Sheriff's Department, under Deputy Brian Coburn.

Coburn, having inherited the case file from Carver, was also inclined to believe Misty was a runaway. In his interactions with Bober, Coburn expressed a dismissive attitude, indicating he wouldn't share any findings with either Bober or Diana, whom he viewed as a troubled individual and a problematic figure in law enforcement, respectively.

Bober continued his investigation, using the threat of media involvement as leverage – a tactic he had found effective in the past. However, the Puyallup police, growing weary of Bober's methods, orchestrated a drug bust against him, leading to potential legal troubles for Bober.

Despite facing the prospect of imprisonment, Bober remained doggedly committed to the case. Meanwhile, a complex tug-of-war developed between Bober and the police, with Diana caught in the middle.

In October, Cory Bober's arrest momentarily hampered his investigation into Misty's disappearance. Seizing this opportunity, the police department, including Sergeant Herm Carver and Deputy Brian Coburn, urged Diana to distance herself from Bober. They portrayed him as detrimental to her search for Misty, possibly driven by their own motives to diminish Bober's influence.

Eventually, they persuaded Diana to file a restraining order against Bober. This move coincided with reactivating Misty's name on the missing persons report, a standard procedure for cases extending beyond 30 days. The restraining order, based on Diana's revelations of Bober's extreme tactics in targeting Randy Achziger, effectively sidelined Bober from the investigation.

However, by early November, Diana rescinded the restraining order. She recognized Bober's role as a supportive figure during her ordeal. Despite his unconventional methods and intense focus on Achziger, Bober had provided Diana with emotional support, connections to support groups, and, crucially, the belief that Misty was not just a runaway. This belief resonated with Diana, and she chose to align with Bober, even though she still harbored suspicions about Rheuban Schmidt.

Bober's determination saw some vindication in November 1992 when King County officials announced the reopening of the Green River Killer case, now linking the murders of two other Puyallup girls, Kim Delange and Anna Chebetnoy, to the serial killings. For Bober, this development reinforced his theory, though Misty's case could not be directly connected without more evidence.

Undeterred, Bober continued his search efforts. He gleaned information about the location where the bodies of the two Puyallup victims had been found and organized search parties in the area, hoping to find any trace of Misty.

On December 2nd, the shift in the official stance was palpable as the Pierce County Sheriffs classified Misty's case as "missing under suspicious circumstances," moving away from the initial runaway label. This change reinvigorated the investigation.

A week later, Bober presented his written theory to the Puyallup investigators and preemptively informed them of an upcoming news story. Published in the News Tribune, the article detailed the search efforts and attempted to link Misty's disappearance to the other Puyallup cases, hoping to provoke a reaction from the perpetrator.

Despite these efforts, no new developments arose. Diana's encounter with Rheuban Schmidt, who fled from her at a grocery store, left her more confused and distraught.

As the bleakness of the situation deepened, Diana faced her darkest moment in December, attempting suicide. Fortunately, she survived, but the pain of her daughter's unresolved disappearance continued to haunt her as she returned to her empty home, with the festive season only amplifying her sense of loss.

In January 1993, an episode of "Northwest Afternoon" aired on KOMO, the local ABC affiliate, featuring Diana along with Trina Brevard, a friend of Misty Copsey. King County Detective Jim Doyon, who had worked on the Green River Killer case and the investigation of two murdered girls from Puyallup, also appeared on the show.

During the broadcast, the phone lines were opened for viewers to share tips and leads. A significant call came in from a woman who claimed to have seen Misty walking down Meridian, the main thoroughfare in Puyallup near the fairgrounds, passing a 7-11 store around ten o'clock. This sighting, if accurate, could shift the timeline of Misty's disappearance by about half an hour. However, the woman who provided this tip was never interviewed by detectives from either Puyallup or Pierce County, and her identity remains unknown. Furthermore, the footage of this episode has been lost over time, unavailable from Bober, Diana, or the KOMO network.

The day after the show aired, Detective Doyon visited a known dump site near Highway 410, around mile marker 30. Although he didn't find any evidence related to Misty's case, his involvement was seen as a positive sign by Diana and Cory Bober, given his experience and interest despite having no jurisdiction in this case.

On January 10th, 1993, four months after Misty's disappearance, a disturbing incident occurred just five blocks from where Misty was last seen. In the early hours, a fifteen-year-old girl walking on Meridian was approached by a man in a Red Camaro. Identified as Robert Leslie Hickey, he made inappropriate comments and forcibly abducted the girl. He took her to a remote area, assaulted her, and then attempted to kill her by throwing her off a ravine. Miraculously, the girl survived.

Hickey was convicted of first-degree assault and sentenced to seven years in prison, with eligibility for early parole. Despite the similarities in his crime to Misty's case and the proximity to her disappearance, Hickey was not investigated as a suspect in Misty's case. He was released from prison after serving five years and would later reoffend.

As Cory Bober delved deeper into the case, he faced a critical moment of self-reflection. Despite his unwavering conviction that he was close to uncovering a crucial lead, tangible results eluded him. Bober had thoroughly investigated the area where two other victims from Puyallup had been discovered, yet nothing significant had surfaced.

In his meticulous pursuit, Bober uncovered that on the night of Misty's disappearance, his primary suspect, Randy Achziger, had a solid alibi. Achziger was near the fairgrounds, at the Puyallup Good Samaritan Hospital, where his sister was giving birth. This revelation prompted Bober to re-evaluate his approach.

A crucial oversight emerged when Bober reconnected with the medical examiner's office. He discovered they had been searching the wrong side of the freeway. The bodies of the previous victims were found on the south side, not the north side where Bober and his team had focused their efforts.

With this new information, Bober intensified preparations for a search planned for Saturday, February 7th. He publicized the event through the media, hoping to draw attention and aid in the search. Despite past disappointments, Bober was convinced this time would be different.

The day of the search arrived, and Bober, along with Diana Smith, led a group through the woods on the south side of Highway 410, near mile marker 30. The search party combed the forest, looking for any trace of Misty.

In a startling discovery, they found the jeans Misty had been wearing the night she vanished. The faded, baggy jeans borrowed from her mother lay in the dark woods, a harrowing find that shattered the persistent rumors of Misty being a runaway.

While the discovery brought a grim satisfaction to Bober, affirming his theories after years of struggle and resistance from law enforcement, it was a devastating blow to Diana. Alongside the jeans were socks and underwear, which Diana confirmed belonged to Misty.

This tragic find marked a turning point for Diana. The faint hope she had clung to, the hope that Misty might still be alive, was now replaced by a crushing reality. Bober's long-held assertions, once a source of contention and skepticism, now resonated with a painful truth. Misty, her beloved daughter, was truly gone.

Detective Jim Doyon of King County, known for his involvement in the Green River Killer case, was assigned to lead the investigation at the Highway 410 site where Misty Copsey's clothes were found. The area fell within his jurisdiction, providing him the authority to oversee the case.

Doyon's first encounter with Cory Bober at the scene was not what he had anticipated. Bober, a young man in his late 20s, appeared physically unimposing but possessed an intense enthusiasm, particularly about the discovery of the clothes. Doyon, an experienced detective, was cautious about Bober's involvement but recognized the significance of his finding.

Doyon observed that the location where Misty's clothes were found differed from the usual dump sites of the killer. Previous victims had been discovered deeper in the woods, whereas Misty's clothes were right off the road in a forested ditch. This discrepancy raised questions for Doyon, especially since he had searched the area recently without finding anything. Forensic analysis suggested the clothes had been there for some time, predating Bober's news story leak.

While Doyon intensified his investigation efforts, including deploying police dogs and arranging for helicopter surveillance with thermal imaging, Diana faced the harsh reality of returning to an empty home, overwhelmed by anger.

She was furious at the police for their perceived inaction, at herself for not being able to protect Misty, and at Bober for revealing such a painful truth.

Meanwhile, Sergeant Herm Carver of the Puyallup Police, upon hearing about the discovery, suspected Bober and Diana of foul play. Simultaneously, he received a tip from Dede Miles, a friend of Misty's, who mentioned Rheuban Schmidt's frequent visits to Misty's house. Schmidt was known to leave before Diana returned home, raising further suspicions.

Despite this new information about Schmidt, Carver remained skeptical of the circumstances surrounding the discovery of Misty's clothing. He and his department continued to operate under the assumption that Misty was likely still alive and potentially a runaway, casting doubt on the significance of the recent findings.

Cory Bober's discovery of Misty Copsey's pants in the woods significantly boosted his confidence in the investigation, leading him to believe he was a pivotal figure in keeping the case alive. In the weeks that followed, Bober worked closely with Pierce County Detective Tim Kobel, guiding him through various theories and potential leads. Bober's suggestions, however, often seemed far-fetched, ranging from speculating Misty's location under a bridge to near a stop sign. He even interpreted random items like shoes hanging on an electric cable as potential signs of the Green River Killer, while continuing to share his theories about Randy Achziger, who had been cleared as a suspect.

Kobel, despite being initially tolerant of Bober's intense approach, found himself embroiled in a series of wild goose chases. Meanwhile, Diana, grappling with the reality of her daughter's disappearance, started to suspect Bober himself, given his keen interest and involvement in finding Misty's clothes.

Bober's involvement in the case took a turn when he faced sentencing for his drug charges. Hoping that his cooperation with the investigation would earn him leniency, Bober pleaded guilty. However, his expectations were shattered at the sentencing. Local police officers testified against him, painting a negative image that led to a fourteen-month jail sentence. This development effectively halted any contribution he might have made to Misty's case, pushing back potential progress.

While incarcerated, Bober was visited by Detective Kobel, who urged him to share any information or evidence he had, particularly regarding his extensive case file against Achziger. Bober, feeling betrayed by the police, vehemently refused to cooperate and threatened to sever all ties with the investigation, insisting on recognition for his efforts rather than handing over his findings to those he believed wrongfully imprisoned him.

With Bober in jail, Detective Jim Doyon of King County became the primary investigator actively pursuing new leads in Misty's case. Doyon conducted an interview with Trina Bevard, Misty's friend and companion at the Puyallup Fair, six months after Misty's disappearance. During this interview, Doyon presented Trina with a photo of Misty's jeans found in the woods, eliciting an emotional response from her.

Trina provided valuable insights, clarifying that their initial plan had been to get a ride from Rheuban Schmidt. However, Schmidt had declined to pick them up, citing a lack of funds and gas. Despite Misty's efforts to convince him, including offering him access to money at her house, Schmidt remained unwilling to help.

Trina also admitted her distrust of Schmidt and had already decided against relying on him for a ride. Her account of the events at the fair aligned with what Diana had previously informed investigators: the girls had separated after 8:30 PM, and she had walked home to Sumner.

Following the airing of a segment on "America's Most Wanted" about Misty Copsey, a new wave of tips flooded in, all directed to the Puyallup detectives and handled by Sergeant Herm Carver. Despite Carver's efforts to dissuade Diana Smith from associating with Cory Bober, who was struggling with his reputation in prison, Diana remained steadfast. She urged Carver to intensify the investigation and suggested looking into Rheuban Schmidt, who had long been her primary suspect.

Carver, though hesitant, decided to investigate Schmidt's background. His inquiry led him to Adam's Ribs, a restaurant where Schmidt occasionally worked. The owner, Frank Rodriguez, shared disturbing statements Schmidt had made about Misty, including claiming to know her burial location and implying the police investigation was missing key details by a significant distance.

When Carver and his team approached Schmidt at his workplace, Schmidt fled, indicating a potential lead. He was later brought in for questioning after initially refusing to speak with the police.

During the interview, Schmidt downplayed his earlier comments as mere attempts to deflect attention. He reiterated his previous claim to Diana that he had not picked up the girls due to a lack of gas. However, a notable detail emerged: Schmidt admitted to experiencing blackouts, including one on the night of September 17th, 1992, that lasted until the next morning. He had no recollection of his activities during this period.

Schmidt woke up the following day with no memory of the previous night's events and inexplicably drove to his grandmother's farm in Buckley. Notably, Buckley is in close proximity to Enumclaw and less than eight miles from where Misty's jeans were discovered.

Despite these alarming revelations, Sergeant Carver remained skeptical of Schmidt being the key suspect. The decision to administer a polygraph test to Schmidt was more a formality than a conviction of his guilt, indicating Carver's continued doubt about Schmidt's involvement in Misty's disappearance.

Cory Bober's determination to keep Misty Copsey's case in the spotlight led to a series of developments. During this time, Sergeant Herm Carver received numerous tips following the airing of a segment on "America's Most Wanted." Despite Carver's attempts to steer Diana Smith away from Bober, she remained convinced of Rheuban Schmidt's potential involvement and urged Carver to investigate him further.

Carver's investigation into Schmidt took an interesting turn when he visited Adam's Ribs, where Schmidt worked. The owner, Frank Rodriguez, shared alarming statements Schmidt had made, including claiming to know where Misty was buried and suggesting that the police were searching in the wrong area. When approached by the police, Schmidt fled, further arousing suspicion.

During Schmidt's polygraph test, he exhibited odd behavior, seemingly trying to lower his physiological responses. Despite the test being inconclusive, partly due to his behavior, the detectives did not pursue further investigations into Schmidt.

Diana later learned that Schmidt had supposedly passed the polygraph. Frustrated, she confronted Bober's suspect, Randy Achziger. However, her suspicion was reignited when Rodriguez called to reiterate the disturbing statements Schmidt had made.

Around this time, the police shifted their focus to a new suspect, Michael Rhyner, following revelations about Trina Bevard's whereabouts on the night of Misty's disappearance. Contrary to her initial statement, Trina had received a ride from her older boyfriend, Michael Rhyner. This new information, coupled with Rhyner's questionable past and connections to previous victims, directed the investigation toward him.

Detectives discovered that Rhyner was selling his car, a blue 1981 Ford Escort. An undercover officer purchased the car, allowing the police to conduct forensic tests in hopes of finding a link to Misty.

The case's complexity deepened with these new developments. The police's initial stance on Misty as a runaway was increasingly challenged, not only by the mounting media attention but also by the involvement of King County Detective Jim Doyon.

In prison, Cory Bober, known for his obsession with the Green River Killer case, faced a challenging environment, sharing a cell with convicted murderer Joseph Duncan. The stress of his situation intensified, leading Bober to write aggressive letters to various contacts, including his parents, Diana, and Detective Kobel. Kobel later speculated that Bober might have been mentally unwell, fixated on the case to an unhealthy extent.

During this period, Bober's long-time suspect, Randy Achziger, was arrested and convicted for molesting two children. While this might have seemed like a form of vindication for Bober, his ultimate goal remained unachieved: proving Achziger was the Green River Killer and gaining recognition for it.

Meanwhile, the investigation shifted focus to Michael Rhyner, whose car was being forensically tested. Sergeant Carver and his team interviewed Rhyner, probing into his history, his relationship with Trina, and his alibi for the night of Misty's disappearance. Rhyner discussed a past juvenile rape accusation, which he had been cleared of. Although the detectives found some of his responses deceptive, Rhyner eventually passed a polygraph test, leading them to rule him out as a suspect.

Attention then returned to Rheuban Schmidt, who became a prime suspect nearly a year after Misty's disappearance. The detectives interviewed James Tinsley, Rheuban's roommate at the time. Tinsley recounted the night Misty vanished, noting that Rheuban left their residence shortly after an argument with his girlfriend and didn't return until midnight. This account contradicted Rheuban's claim of a blackout and not remembering his whereabouts.

Tinsley also expressed his belief that Rheuban was capable of violence and had a temper, adding weight to the suspicions against him. However, when Rheuban was brought in for questioning and another polygraph, he slightly altered his statement but maintained the essence of his original account. Despite the suspicions and the new information provided by Tinsley, Rheuban passed the polygraph test.

With his car no longer available for forensic testing and having passed the polygraph, Rheuban was released by the police and was never again investigated as a suspect in Misty Copsey's disappearance.

Following the exclusion of Rheuban Schmidt as a suspect, Sergeant Herm Carver shifted his focus to Diana, Misty's mother, despite her seemingly having a solid alibi and being the one who reported Misty missing.

Carver's renewed scrutiny of Diana involved questioning her, requesting polygraph tests, and delving into her past by speaking with her former parole officer and ex-boyfriends. Although Diana appeared to pass the polygraph, Carver shared his doubts about her honesty with other investigators, including King County's Detective Jim Doyon. Carver had long harbored suspicions that Diana, along with Cory Bober, had planted the pants found near Highway 410 as part of a cover-up.

Bober, having been released from prison and on work release, was also a focus of Carver's suspicion. Scheduled for a polygraph test in March 1994, Bober failed to show up, citing mistrust in the process and fearing it would be used to incriminate him falsely.

As time passed, the case seemed to stagnate. The Puyallup Police continued to promote the theory that Misty was a runaway. In 1996, they collaborated with Misty's estranged father, Buck Copsey, anticipating a call from Misty on her eighteenth birthday, which never materialized. The runaway narrative persisted.

In 1997, Bober faced charges of marijuana dealing but chose to contest them vehemently, viewing them as an attempt by the Puyallup police to silence him. Remarkably, after a prolonged legal battle spanning over two years, Bober emerged victorious. His defense unexpectedly yielded a critical piece of evidence: the forensic results from the analysis of Misty's pants, conducted back in 1993.

Bober's scrutiny of the forensic report revealed the presence of hairs, fibers, and notably, three red paint chips on or near the pants. He seized upon this detail, attempting to link it to Randy Achziger's red Porsche, the suspect he had long pursued.

On May 14, 2001, a disturbing incident unfolded in Lakewood, about ten miles from Puyallup. A 24-year-old woman was walking home from church when she encountered Robert Leslie Hickey, a man previously convicted of a serious offense and released five years into his seven-year sentence.

Hickey, driving a white pickup truck, offered her a ride, which she declined. Undeterred, he stopped the truck and approached her under the pretense of asking for a cigarette. When she refused and attempted to call 911, Hickey attacked her, pushing her down an embankment and assaulting her. However, he fled upon realizing she was dialing for help. The woman managed to call the police, leading to Hickey's arrest and subsequent conviction for attempted second-degree rape. This being his second serious offense, he was sentenced to life in prison without parole.

Hickey's history and proximity to the area where Misty Copsey disappeared raised questions about his possible involvement in her case and the earlier Puyallup disappearances. There was speculation about the red paint chips found on Misty's pants and whether they could be linked to Hickey's Red Camaro, which he owned at the time.

Meanwhile, in another development, Gary Ridgway was arrested on November 30, 2001, as the Green River Killer, closing a long-standing mystery. For Cory Bober, this was a difficult pill to swallow. Convinced that Randy Achziger was the real culprit, Bober refused to accept Ridgway's guilt, despite Ridgway's confession to numerous murders.

Detective Jim Doyon, who had been involved in the search for the Green River Killer, played a role in Ridgway's arrest. However, the connection between Ridgway and the Puyallup victims, including Misty Copsey, remained unclear. Ridgway had a solid alibi for the day of Misty's disappearance, working his day job. Additionally, Ridgway's plea deal in King County, which spared him the death penalty in exchange for helping locate his victims, meant he had little incentive to confess to any crimes in Pierce County.

To this day, the possibility of linking Ridgway to the Pierce County crimes largely hinges on a potential death-bed confession, as admitting to crimes across county lines could threaten his life.

Despite Gary Ridgeway's arrest as the Green River Killer, Cory Bober remained fixated on his original suspect, Randy Achziger, and continued his efforts to prove Achziger's guilt.

In 2000, Diana Smith, grappling with the unresolved fate of her daughter, had Misty legally declared dead. A funeral was organized, with Bober's assistance, to honor Misty's memory. During this time, Bober's persistence in connecting Achziger to Misty's case led to the testing of paint chips found with her jeans, which ultimately yielded inconclusive results. Additionally, the samples disappeared, further complicating the investigation.

Bober, released from prison and determined to continue his quest, found himself increasingly isolated. His aggressive approach and eccentric theories distanced him from those who once supported him, including Diana Smith. His alibi for the night of Misty's disappearance and lack of a driver's license made him an unlikely suspect, yet his behavior raised concerns.

The hair samples found with Misty's jeans were tested in 2013 but did not match any known individuals, leaving their significance unclear. The Puyallup Police Department, recognizing the shortcomings of the initial investigation, sought public assistance, asking for photographs from the Puyallup Fair on the day Misty disappeared. A tip about Misty getting into a car with a man in a yellow Chrysler Cordoba was unearthed but had not been pursued at the time.

Rheuban Schmidt, another suspect in the case, faced legal troubles unrelated to Misty's disappearance, including theft and domestic violence allegations. A mysterious online posting in 2015 implicated him in Misty's case, but the claims could not be substantiated.

As the years passed, Bober and Diana Smith's relationship deteriorated. Bober's social media presence, marked by outlandish claims and conspiracy theories, further alienated him from credible investigation efforts. Despite his persistence, his theories about Achziger and his bizarre allegations about Aleister Crowley did not gain traction with law enforcement.

Meanwhile, Diana Smith continued to seek closure for her daughter's disappearance, appearing on local shows and holding onto the belief that Schmidt was involved in some way. The truth about what happened to Misty remains elusive, a haunting mystery that continues to affect all those connected to the case.

Murder of Adrian Donohoe

drian Donohoe's life was a rich tapestry of family, community, and public service, woven deeply into the fabric of Irish society. Born into a close-knit family on January 14, 1972, in the picturesque surroundings of Kilnaleck, County Cavan, Adrian was the cherished son of Peggy and Hugh Donohoe. He spent his childhood on the family's bustling farm, where the values of hard work and camaraderie were instilled in him from an early age. Alongside his three brothers - Alan, Colm, and Martin, and two sisters - Anne and Mary, Adrian's early years were filled with the joys and challenges of rural life.

A towering figure, both in stature and character, Adrian stood at an impressive 6 ft 4 in. His athletic prowess shone through in his passion for Gaelic football. Adrian wasn't just a player; he was a force on the field, playing midfield for his local club with a blend of grace and power. His skill and dedication saw him ascend to represent Cavan GAA at the Under-21 level, a testament to his talent and commitment to the sport.

Education played a pivotal role in Adrian's formative years. He attended local primary and secondary schools, where he was known for his friendly nature and leadership qualities. In 1994, a new chapter began in Adrian's life when he joined the Garda Síochána, Ireland's national police service. This career choice was a family tradition, with two of his brothers also donning the Garda uniform.

It was at the Garda Síochána College in Templemore, County Tipperary, that Adrian's personal and professional lives intertwined. Here, he met Caroline, the woman who would become his wife. Caroline, hailing from County Clare, shared Adrian's commitment to public service, with her own family also serving in the Gardaí. She was stationed with the Garda National Immigration Bureau at Dundalk Garda Station – the very place where Adrian worked.

Together, Adrian and Caroline built a life filled with love, dedication, and service. They were blessed with two young children, a boy and a girl, who were 6 and 7 years old respectively at the time of Adrian's tragic passing. The couple's deep roots in the community were evident in their involvement with local activities. Adrian was more than just a police officer; he was a "father figure" in his community, passionately playing and coaching for his local GAA club, St Patrick's GFC, on the Cooley Peninsula.

Adrian's professional journey with the Garda Síochána was marked by dedication and distinction. He served his entire 19-year career in Dundalk, where he rose through the ranks to become a detective, a role in which he served with honor and integrity. The Donohoe family resided just 4 km from the site of the tragic incident that took Adrian's life. Their children attended Bellurgan National School, poignantly located directly across the road from where the incident occurred.

On the evening of Friday, January 25, 2013, a somber episode unfolded, involving Detective Garda Adrian Donohoe and his colleague Detective Garda Joe Ryan. Engaged in a routine cash escort, the two detectives found themselves in the midst of a critical situation that would leave an indelible mark on their lives and the broader community.

The setting was a typical Irish evening, and the two detectives were en route for a significant operation. Driving an unmarked silver Ford Mondeo, Ryan took the wheel, with both detectives in civilian attire, subtly armed with concealed 9mm SIG Sauer P226 sidearms – a standard issue for members of the Garda

Síochána's armed units. It's worth noting that while the Garda Síochána is primarily an unarmed force, certain units are equipped with firearms, and a notable proportion of the force, up to 25%, is authorized to carry weapons.

Their mission was to rendezvous with officials from local credit unions, including those from Omeath, Cooley, and the Lordship Credit Union in Bellurgan. The plan was to form a three-car convoy and transport the day's takings to a bank in Dundalk town, depositing them in a night safe. This protocol, recently upgraded from an unarmed, uniformed Garda escort to an armed, plain-clothes detective escort, was a response to a robbery 18 months prior at the credit union, where €62,000 was stolen without any casualties.

The scene at the Lordship Credit Union car park was quiet and unassuming as they arrived around 9:30 pm. Donohoe and Ryan parked their vehicle, aligning it next to a car from another credit union branch and the car belonging to Lordship officials. Suddenly, the tranquility was shattered. A navy-blue Volkswagen Passat, previously stationed on the road's hard shoulder, moved to block the entrance. Four balaclava-clad members of a gang, who had been concealed behind a nearby wall, revealed themselves, while a fifth member drove the Passat.

As Donohoe stepped out of the car to investigate, a tragedy struck. He was shot in the back of the head at close range with a long-barreled shotgun by one of the masked assailants. The shot, fired in the darkness, was sudden and fatal. Before Ryan could comprehend the situation fully, he found himself at gunpoint, forced out of his vehicle and onto the ground by gang members armed with a shotgun, handgun, and a hammer. The officers were caught off guard, with no opportunity to use their own weapons.

The raiders then turned their attention to the credit union officials' car, containing approximately €40,000 in cash and cheques. In a hurried and chaotic moment, they seized a bag containing only €4,000, overlooking the larger sum. Ryan and the credit union staff, though physically unharmed, were left in shock as the gang fled, taking Ryan's car keys to delay any immediate pursuit.

The aftermath was a scene of desperation and urgency. Despite Ryan's frantic efforts to save his colleague, emergency services pronounced Donohoe dead upon their arrival. An extensive manhunt ensued, with Garda Headquarters mobilizing all available units and coordinating with the Police Service of Northern Ireland. The suspects, however, had already crossed into Northern Ireland before the border could be effectively secured. A Garda helicopter, with special permission, briefly entered UK airspace, complemented by a PSNI helicopter in the search operations north of the border.

Approximately an hour following the tragic events at the credit union, a critical discovery was made. At 10:30 pm, on that fateful Friday, January 25, 2013, authorities located a vehicle, burnt-out and abandoned, on Cumsons Road in Newtownhamilton. This secluded, forest-lined laneway, nestled between the villages of Darkley and Keady in south County Armagh, Northern Ireland, instantly became a significant focus of the investigation.

The Police Service of Northern Ireland promptly initiated an exhaustive technical examination of both the vehicle and the area. The car, a 2008 Volkswagen Passat with a distinctive "graphite navy blue" color, was registered in Dublin and had automatic transmission. Detectives soon linked this vehicle to the murder at the credit union. It was established that the car had been stolen earlier in the week, specifically between the late hours of Tuesday, January 22, and the early morning of Wednesday, January 23, from the Clogherhead area in County Louth.

In the unfolding investigation, Gardaí and the PSNI speculated that the criminals likely used another getaway vehicle to escape after setting the Passat ablaze. The number of suspects involved in the overall crime was believed to be more than five.

The Garda Technical Bureau, with assistance from the Divisional Scenes of Crime Unit, conducted a meticulous forensic examination at the crime scene over three days. Additionally, the Divisional Search Team was deployed to meticulously scour the vicinity. Among the items recovered was a hammer, used by the perpetrators to break the window of one of the credit union cars.

The incident necessitated a thorough medical examination. Deputy State Pathologist Khalid Jaber conducted an autopsy at Our Lady of Lourdes Hospital in Drogheda, after initially examining the body at the scene.

As protocol dictates in such grave circumstances involving a Garda, the Garda Síochána Ombudsman Commission was promptly notified. GSOC officials visited the scene as part of their investigative duties.

In the days following Detective Garda Adrian Donohoe's death, Garda Commissioner Martin Callinan, who later retired in March 2014, attended a case conference at Dundalk Garda Station. An incident room was established there for the ongoing investigation. Demonstrating the gravity of the situation, Commissioner Callinan announced that 150 senior detectives would be dedicated to the case. This formidable team included personnel from the National specialist units such as the Special Detective Unit, National Bureau of Criminal Investigation, and Organised Crime Unit. Additionally, the force's armed intervention teams, the Emergency Response Unit and Regional Support Unit, were placed on high alert.

The scale of this investigation was unprecedented, involving over 1,000 Garda officers, making it one of the largest criminal investigations in the history of the state.

In their rigorous investigation into the shooting and robbery that led to Detective Donohoe's death, Gardaí identified a group of five males directly involved in the incident. These individuals were part of a larger criminal gang known to operate in the border area. Following the attack, it was believed that the culprits fled to Northern Ireland, where they possibly remained hidden for several weeks. The primary suspect, considered the leader of this five-person gang, was a young man from the Crossmaglen area in south Armagh. Intriguingly, he was allegedly acquainted with Detective Donohoe, suggesting a potential motive for the murder. However, it's noteworthy that Donohoe was not initially assigned to the credit union cash escort and had only taken over the shift in a late change with another officer.

Over a month after the tragedy, in late February, the Gardaí convened a press briefing at their Dublin Metropolitan Region Headquarters on Harcourt Street. During this event, they renewed their appeal for information and presented two key pieces of evidence to the media for the first time. One was a unique hammer found at the crime scene, characterized by a black rubber handle, red painted section, and a soft rubber head, typically used in panel beating or motorcycle repairs. The other was a distinctive green "Cosatto" children's car booster seat with a "Little Monster" motif, which had been in the stolen vehicle. Authorities believed this booster seat, suitable for babies and young children and priced at €119, might have been removed from the car before the murder and subsequently discarded, sold, or given away.

By mid-April, the joint efforts of Gardaí and the PSNI had led to a public appeal for information about a white Heavy Goods Vehicle seen on Shean Road, Forkhill, Armagh on the night of the murder. This truck, which might have been experiencing a breakdown, was reported to have had several individuals around it. Both police forces were eager to speak with anyone connected to this vehicle, whether as the owner, repair service, or as a witness to any activity involving the truck that night.

On the first anniversary of Detective Donohoe's death, Garda Commissioner Martin Callinan visited Dundalk Garda Station to provide an update on the inquiry. He affirmed the commitment to justice and highlighted the international scope of the investigation, involving collaboration with police forces and law enforcement agencies from the United Kingdom, Netherlands,

United States, and Australia, alongside Europol and Interpol. Callinan also commended the PSNI for their significant role in the investigation. By this time, over 4,000 investigative tasks had been completed, including 4,000 lines of inquiry, 2,100 statements, interviews with over 800 people, review of 400,000 hours of CCTV footage, collection of 1,200 evidence exhibits, and more than 30 search warrants executed.

Nóirín O'Sullivan, who succeeded Callinan as Garda Commissioner, expressed her firm belief in April 2014 that justice would be served for Adrian Donohoe.

The tragic passing of Adrian Donohoe resonated deeply across Ireland, drawing strong condemnation from the highest levels of government and stirring profound emotions among the public. Ireland's President, Michael D. Higgins, and the Taoiseach at the time, Enda Kenny, were among the first to express their dismay and condemnation of the crime. Cabinet ministers from both the Republic of Ireland and Northern Ireland also voiced their denunciations, unified in their stance against the violence.

The Minister for Justice, Alan Shatter, highlighted the premeditated nature of the murder, noting the attackers' awareness of the police presence at the credit union and the ambush that followed. He issued a stern warning to the perpetrators, emphasizing the mandatory 40-year prison sentence for killing a member of the Garda, irrespective of who actually fired the fatal shot. Commissioner Martin Callinan, echoing this sentiment, pledged an unwavering commitment to tracking down and capturing those responsible. The PSNI, under the leadership of Chief Constable Matt Baggott, also promised full cooperation and support in the pursuit of justice.

The impact of Donohoe's death extended far beyond political statements, deeply affecting the Irish public and being perceived as a national tragedy. The incident brought back memories of the last Garda officer shot and killed in the line of duty, Detective Garda Jerry McCabe, who was fatally wounded in June 1996 in County Limerick by the Provisional Irish Republican Army.

Jerry McCabe's widow, Anne McCabe, extended her heartfelt sympathy to the Donohoe family. In a poignant gesture, retired Detective Garda Ben O'Sullivan, who survived the attack that claimed McCabe's life, signed a book of condolence for Donohoe's family, friends, and colleagues.

In an effort to assist the investigation, the Irish television programme "Crimecall" on RTÉ featured Superintendent David Taylor from the Garda Press Office, who made a public appeal for assistance in solving the case. The public's response to Donohoe's death was overwhelming, with a Facebook tribute page amassing over 40,000 signatures in just a few days. The Irish League of Credit Unions also stepped forward, offering a €50,000 reward for information leading to arrests and prosecutions, an amount later augmented by Crimestoppers with a significant five-figure sum.

A special tribute was paid to Donohoe on 18 May 2013, during the annual Garda Memorial Day service at Dublin Castle, where his family was presented with a special Garda remembrance medal. The medal was awarded to his widow, Caroline, commemorating all 87 members of the Gardaí who had fallen in the line of duty.

In September 2013, eight months following his untimely death, Donohoe was posthumously honored with a People of the Year Award for his bravery and courage. The award, presented in Citywest, Dublin by GAA personality Mícheál Ó Muircheartaigh, was accepted by Caroline Donohoe. In her acceptance speech, she lovingly remembered Adrian as "the love of my life" and "the best father any child could have," vowing to miss him "every minute of every day as long as I live."

In late February 2013, the Gardaí executed six carefully planned searches in the Dundalk area as part of their ongoing investigation. During these operations, two individuals, a father and son aged in their 70s and 30s respectively, were apprehended under the Offences against the State Acts 1939–1998, a set of laws pertaining to terrorism. They were detained at Drogheda Garda Station, where the legislation allowed them to be held for up to seven days without formal charges.

A Garda spokesperson clarified that these arrests were part of a broader crackdown on criminal and potentially subversive activities in the region, but they were not directly linked to Donohoe's murder. After two days in custody, both individuals were released, and a file regarding their case was forwarded to the Director of Public Prosecutions for evaluation of potential charges. The suspicion was that these men might have been involved in a vehicle theft ring, potentially providing stolen cars to other criminals, including the vehicle used in Donohoe's murder.

In early April 2013, the Gardaí conducted several targeted raids in County Louth. In Hackballscross, Dundalk, they seized mobile phones and laptops during a property search. Another raid in Kilsaran, Castlebellingham, resulted in the confiscation of firearms, explosives, and illegal drugs. While no arrests were made, these operations were aimed at disrupting criminal networks in the border regions between County Louth and County Armagh, including those believed to be connected to Donohoe's murder. These locations underwent extensive forensic examinations following the searches.

That same month, the PSNI's Special Operations Branch, known for their heavily armed personnel, raided four houses in south County Armagh. This operation led to the seizure of mobile phones, documentation, and other materials for forensic analysis. Senior PSNI officers indicated that these searches were intelligence-led, targeting suspected criminals or associates of the gang implicated in Donohoe's murder. Although no arrests were made during these searches, the primary aim was to collect evidence pertinent to the ongoing investigation.

Further follow-up operations were conducted a few weeks later by Gardaí south of the border. In the Carlingford area of Louth, several search warrants were executed, continuing the extensive investigative efforts across jurisdictional boundaries.

In early May 2013, the Gardaí undertook numerous searches in the town of Faughart, near Dundalk. These operations involved various specialized units, including the Emergency Response Unit, Regional Support Unit, National Bureau of Criminal Investigation, Garda Stolen Motor Vehicle Investigation Unit, Divisional Search Team, and the Divisional Scenes of Crime Unit. However, the Garda Press Office did not reveal the outcomes of these searches, citing operational reasons for the secrecy.

Throughout the investigation, a focused effort by both the Gardaí and the PSNI led to the identification of five primary suspects. These individuals were believed to have been directly involved in both the fatal shooting of the 41-year-old father of two and the subsequent robbery at the scene. The suspects were all young males, hailing from the vicinity of the Louth-Armagh border, and were thought to be part of a larger criminal gang consisting of approximately 15 to 20 members. This gang was known to have connections with dissident republican paramilitary and terror organizations through family ties and acquaintances. Several among these suspects had prior criminal records and were implicated in other criminal activities.

One of the suspects, identified as the presumed leader of the gang and the shooter, was a male in his early 20s from Crossmaglen, County Armagh. He was notably associated with the Crossmaglen Rangers Gaelic Athletic Club. Among the group were also a pair of brothers. Despite their identification, immediate arrests were not made as the Gardaí aimed to build a comprehensive, "watertight" case before proceeding with apprehensions. Given the gravity of the crime, suspects charged with murder or conspiracy to murder a serving member of the Garda Síochána could potentially face trial in the non-jury Special Criminal Court in Dublin, with the possibility of a 40-year sentence in Portlaoise Prison, a maximum-security facility.

In the aftermath of the murder, some suspects provided prepared statements to the police on both sides of the border, with legal representation present, and were subsequently questioned under caution.

In a significant development in March 2013, the primary suspect in Donohoe's murder reportedly fled to the United States. This individual, a man in his 20s from south Armagh, traveled from Northern Ireland to mainland Britain and then flew to New York City using a British passport. At the time, there was no arrest warrant against him, which allowed him to travel unhindered. However, this suspect was due in court in Ireland for unrelated offenses prior to the Bellurgan incident and failed to appear. Upon his arrival in the U.S., Irish authorities alerted American security services to his presence. The New York City Police Department, the Federal Bureau of Investigation, and the United States Marshals Service were all informed of his identity and tasked with monitoring his whereabouts. Additionally, Garda detectives traveled to the U.S. to assist in tracking the suspect's movements. Despite these circumstances, he was granted a holiday visa upon entering the country.

It was understood that another accomplice had fled to Boston in April, eventually reuniting with the prime suspect in New York. Further complicating matters, the prime suspect's girlfriend, who herself was under investigation for providing an alibi for her boyfriend on the night of the murder, traveled to New York in September. She had initially given her statement to the PSNI. U.S. authorities were closely monitoring the movements of these individuals.

By December 2013, two suspects linked to the murder investigation found themselves compelled to provide statements in New York. Senior detectives from the Garda National Bureau of Criminal Investigation, along with U.S. law enforcement officials, brought these two individuals in for questioning from a property in New York. Despite their refusal to answer questions, U.S. legal provisions required them to submit written witness statements about the incident. These suspects, Irish males in their early 20s, had relocated to the U.S. following Donohoe's murder. Reports indicated that they were in the U.S. on Green Card visas at the time.

Meanwhile, two other male suspects had traveled to Australia, one in April 2013 and another in June 2013, presumably to evade prosecution. Suspected of involvement in the shooting and robbery, they remained unarrested as no warrants had been issued. In January 2014, Gardaí detectives visited Sydney, compelling one of these suspects to provide a statement to authorities. It was reported that upon the expiration of his visa, he faced deportation if he did not voluntarily leave Australia, with Australian police keeping an eye on his activities.

Back in Northern Ireland, another suspect in his early 20s from County Down remained under scrutiny. He was interrogated by the PSNI regarding his involvement in the crime and was later prosecuted for an unrelated rape charge.

In a significant development in October 2016, the fiancée of one of the suspected killers was arrested in the U.S. on immigration offenses. This action followed a request from Gardaí for her extradition to Ireland to face charges. She was subsequently deported to Ireland in January, further expanding the international scope of the investigation into Donohoe's murder.

On May 18, 2017, a pivotal moment occurred in the investigation into Garda Donohoe's murder. The primary suspect in the case was detained in New York by U.S. Immigration and Customs Enforcement agents for violating immigration laws and was subsequently deported to Ireland. This arrest, a result of coordinated efforts between Irish and U.S. law enforcement agencies, was expedited due to its nature as a deportation rather than an extradition. U.S. authorities had been monitoring the suspect's movements at the behest of the Gardaí, and the U.S. Embassy in Dublin acknowledged the sustained collaboration between Gardaí and U.S. officials in this matter. This development was hailed as a major breakthrough by senior Garda officers.

Upon his return to Ireland, the individual faced immediate legal challenges. He was arrested and appeared before a judge, having previously failed to attend court for convictions related to different charges.

Further aiding the investigation, a former associate of the suspect, currently residing in Ireland, began cooperating with the detectives, providing them with potentially valuable information.

The investigation continued to gain momentum when, on February 25, 2018, the individual considered the "chief suspect" in the murder – a 27-year-old man – was arrested. The apprehension occurred at 7:15 pm outside Wheatfield Prison, just as he completed a sentence for unrelated road traffic offenses. He was taken to Dundalk Garda Station for questioning, where he was held for a period of seven days. This detention period was extended following a successful application by the Gardaí to the District Court.

Additionally, on February 26, 2018, a second man, in his 50s, was arrested in Dundalk and detained at Balbriggan Garda Station. After his period of detention, he was released, and a file was prepared for the Director of Public Prosecutions, suggesting that his involvement was still under consideration by the authorities.

On March 4, 2018, Aaron Brady, 27, from New Road, Crossmaglen, County Armagh, faced charges at a special sitting of Dundalk District Court for the capital murder of Detective Garda Adrian Donohoe during his duty. Detective Inspector Pat Marry stated that Brady strongly denied any involvement in the murder when charged. He was then remanded in custody, with a scheduled court appearance at Cloverhill District Court on March 9.

The court appearance saw heightened security, with a significant Garda presence and members of the public gathering. Notably, representatives from the US Department of Homeland Security were also in attendance.

This development came after extensive collaboration between Gardaí and US authorities, particularly with the Homeland Security Investigations of the US

Immigration and Customs Enforcement. Their joint investigation revealed that Brady had been living in New York, entering the United States under the Visa Waiver Program but overstaying, thereby violating immigration rules. He was arrested by HSI New York and ICE's Enforcement and Removal Operations in May 2017 for his expired visa, and was eventually deported back to Ireland, where he was arrested by Garda Detectives.

Alysa D. Erichs, Acting Deputy Executive Associate Director of HSI, emphasized the United States' commitment to not being a safe haven for those who harm law enforcement officers. She highlighted the collaborative effort with Gardaí and the significance of Brady's deportation and arrest.

Meanwhile, reports indicated that the remaining suspected gang members were believed to be in the US, Australia, and Northern Ireland, with thousands of lines of inquiry still being pursued by Gardaí.

On August 10, 2020, Brady was found guilty of robbery at the Lordship Credit Union in 2013, and two days later, he was also convicted of the capital murder of Detective Garda Donohoe. He was sentenced to the mandatory 40 years' imprisonment for capital murder, with a potential for earlier release on good behavior in August 2050. On October 14, 2020, Brady was given a life sentence, to serve a minimum of 40 years, and a concurrent 14-year sentence for robbery. He has since applied to appeal his conviction, with a trial date set for October 2023 at the Court of Appeal.

Brady's father, asserting his son's innocence, has initiated a campaign via social media to overturn the conviction.

Following Brady's conviction, the Serious Crime Review Team within the National Bureau of Criminal Investigation arrested eight suspects for alleged witness intimidation and perverting the course of justice during Brady's trial. This action was taken after attempts to intimidate key witnesses, including a video posted online threatening a witness. The trial judge described this as an egregious contempt of court.

In April 2021, detectives recommended charging Aaron Brady for witness intimidation during the Donohoe murder trial. The Court of Appeal, consisting of Mr Justice Edwards, Ms Justice Isobel Kennedy, and Ms Justice Tara Burns, began hearing Brady's appeal on October 4, 2023. Brady's legal team presented 47 grounds of appeal, including concerns about the original trial's timing during the Covid lockdown, non-disclosure of witnesses' immigration statuses, and issues with evidence handling and jury instruction.

On July 15, 2021, 33-year-old Brendan Treanor faced charges at Dundalk District Court for his involvement in the robbery of €7,000 from the Lordship Credit Union in Bellurgan on January 25, 2013. He was also charged with conspiracy to commit burglaries aimed at stealing car keys between September 11, 2012, and January 23, 2013. Following the charges, Treanor was remanded in custody to Cloverhill Prison.

On the same day, 30-year-old James Patrick Gerard Flynn, also known as "Jimmy Flynn," was apprehended in England by the National Crime Agency. The arrest was made following an extradition request from Gardaí in Dublin. Flynn was subsequently extradited from the UK on July 29, 2022, and charged with the same offenses as Treanor, leading to his remand in custody.

Both Flynn and Treanor were later transferred to the Special Criminal Court for a joint trial, scheduled to begin in January 2023.

The trial commenced on February 1, 2023, at the non-jury Special Criminal Court in Dublin, presided over by Mr Justice Tony Hunt, Judge Sarah Berkeley, and Judge Alan Mitchell. The prosecution, led by Lorcan Staines, presented a case built on circumstantial evidence, including cell site analysis and CCTV footage, to establish a pattern of burglaries linked to the accused.

During the trial, key witness testimonies were heard, including that of

Treanor's ex-girlfriend, who recounted speaking with him on the night of the robbery. Her testimony was corroborated by CCTV footage from a Crossmaglen fast-food restaurant, supporting her timeline. Additionally, the ex-housemate of Aaron Brady was treated as a hostile witness during cross-examination, with his statements regarding the whereabouts of Brady and Flynn on the night of the robbery coming under scrutiny.

The prosecution also presented a tattoo on Brendan Treanor's back as circumstantial evidence, linking it to the robbery at Lordship. The tattoo depicted a woman wearing a balaclava and men dressed as 1950s gangsters, alongside a BMW X5, banknotes, bullets, and a knuckle duster.

Closing statements focused on the prosecution's narrative of the involvement of Flynn and Treanor in the robbery and subsequent events, while the defense argued the lack of direct evidence placing their clients at the crime scenes.

The verdicts were delivered on September 11, 2023. James Flynn was found guilty of stealing the keys of a car allegedly used in the robbery and murder but was acquitted of the robbery charge at the Credit Union due to insufficient evidence placing him at the scene. Brendan Treanor was acquitted of all charges, with the court finding no evidence to suggest his presence at the relevant crime scenes. However, Mr Justice Hunt noted clear evidence of Treanor's affiliation with a criminal gang.

On December 21, 2023, James Flynn was sentenced to 8 years in prison for his role in stealing the car keys used in the 2013 armed robbery at the Lordship Credit Union.

Murders of John and Joyce Sheridan

ohn Sheridan's illustrious career is a remarkable tapestry of public
service, legal expertise, and transformative leadership in New Jersey.
A stalwart Republican, Sheridan's journey in state government reached
its zenith in the 1970s, culminating with his pivotal role as Transportation
Commissioner under Governor Thomas Kean from 1982 to 1985. During this
tenure, he masterminded the significant transition of New Jersey's commuter
rail service from the federal entity Conrail to the state-operated New Jersey
Transit Rail Operations. His expertise in transportation and governance was
not only recognized but also sought after, as evidenced by his invaluable
contributions to the transition teams of Republican Governors Christine Todd
Whitman and Chris Christie.

Sheridan's personal life was as fulfilling as his professional endeavors.
Settling in Skillman, an elite enclave in Montgomery Township, Somerset
County, he and his wife Joyce nurtured a family, raising four sons - twins
Mark and Matt, and their siblings Dan and Jim, in this serene suburb not far
from Princeton. Mark Sheridan, emulating his father's professional footsteps,
ascended to the rank of senior partner at Squire Patton Boggs and served as
the chief counsel to New Jersey's Republican Party.

In a striking career shift in 2005, John Sheridan took the reins as the CEO of
Cooper University Hospital in Camden. In tandem with George Norcross,
a significant Democratic figure in South Jersey and the chairman of the
hospital's board, Sheridan steered the hospital's expansion into the renowned

Cooper Health System. This expansion heralded the establishment of pivotal institutions like a four-year medical college and a cancer center, marking a significant milestone in the region's healthcare landscape.

Sheridan's impact extended beyond healthcare. As chair of the Camden non-profit Cooper's Ferry Partnership, he played a strategic role in urban redevelopment. CFP's notable project, the 17-acre L3 site on Camden's waterfront, was a linchpin in the city's revitalization plans. The site's potential transformation into a lucrative office space hub was in line with a state law aimed at fostering economic growth in Camden, New Jersey's most economically distressed city. However, in early 2014, a power struggle within the CFP and the Norcross family led to a reshuffling in the organization's leadership and the subsequent sale of the L3 site to developers linked to the Norcross family, a development Sheridan had endeavored to avert.

As 2014 progressed, Sheridan faced mounting pressure to distance himself from the L3 deal. Allegations surfaced, suggesting a conflict of interest due to his dual roles as CEO of both the hospital and CFP. This controversy, as asserted by his son Mark, was magnified beyond proportion, emphasizing that the hospital's interest in L3 was limited to leasing space rather than outright acquisition. Sheridan's story, therefore, is not just one of notable achievements and significant contributions to New Jersey's political, legal, and healthcare sectors, but also of navigating complex challenges and conflicts in the pursuit of public service and urban development.

In the early hours of September 28, 2014, as dawn was just breaking, a distressing incident unfolded at the Sheridan residence on Meadow Run Drive. Emergency services, including local police and firefighters, were summoned to the scene following reports of a fire. Upon arrival, they discovered smoke billowing from a section of the second floor, specifically emanating from the master bedroom. The firefighters, gaining entry through the unlocked front door, ascended to the upper floor where they swiftly extinguished a fire. This fire, it was discovered, had been intensified by gasoline used as an accelerant.

Amidst the aftermath, a tragic discovery was made. The bodies of John and Joyce Sheridan were found on the floor, both facing upwards. John was declared deceased at the scene, while Joyce was pronounced dead after being transported to the University Medical Center of Princeton at Plainsboro.

Near the scene, investigators found the gasoline can used in the fire, matches, and knives. Adding to the grim scene, a heavy wooden armoire, partially damaged by the fire, had toppled onto John's body, obstructing the door and causing multiple rib fractures. Joyce had sustained first- and second-degree burns across various parts of her body, and both had suffered stab wounds.

The extent of Joyce's injuries was severe. She had been stabbed 12 times, predominantly on her head and hands. Barry Jansen, a police photographer, described her condition as "mutilated". A critical wound that had penetrated her aorta was identified as the cause of death, leading to her death being classified as a homicide. John, in contrast, had five stab wounds, primarily located on his neck and torso. One of these wounds had severed his jugular vein, which would have proved fatal without immediate medical intervention. An autopsy revealed soot in John's lungs and elevated carbon monoxide levels in his blood, indicating he was alive when the fire began. The medical examiner, however, deferred the cause of death pending further investigation.

A week following this tragic event, a memorial service was held for John and Joyce Sheridan at Patriot's Theater in the Trenton War Memorial. The ceremony was attended by their grieving family, hundreds of mourners, and several dignitaries, including Governor Christie, former Governors Thomas Kean, Christie Whitman, and Democrat Jim Florio. The service was a tribute to the Sheridans, with many public officials commemorating John Sheridan's impactful career and contributions, particularly to the city of Camden. George Norcross remarked on how John Sheridan's vision had transformed Camden. The actual funeral was a private affair. At the time of the service, the full details surrounding the couple's demise were not publicly known, though it was disclosed that the fire had been deliberately set.

From the very outset, the investigation into the Sheridan tragedy was marked by tension and conflict between the investigators and the Sheridan family. The grim discovery at the Sheridan residence on the morning of September 28, 2014, set off a complex chain of events.

Matt Sheridan, who lived with his parents but was away on a fishing trip at Fishers Island, New York, was the first family member to be notified by the responding firefighters. He immediately began his journey home and informed his twin brother Mark of the situation. Mark was in New York City, celebrating his wedding anniversary, and upon receiving the news, he and his wife rushed to his parents' home in Skillman, only to be met with the distressing sight of the house cordoned off with crime scene tape.

During his drive to Skillman, Mark picked up his brother Tim and learned that Somerset County prosecutor Geoffrey Soriano was already at the scene. Mark, familiar with the political and legal landscape due to his role as chief counsel for the state GOP, reached out to Chris Porrino, then-chief counsel to Governor Christie, for assistance. Soriano contacted Mark en route, informing him of the suspected arson and the fatal stabbings.

The Sheridan sons were then interviewed at the police station. During this process, detectives asked to search Matt's car, to which he consented. This search led to the discovery of a small amount of cocaine, a digital scale, and plastic bags with traces of white powder, resulting in Matt's arrest, although charges were not immediately filed.

Initially, the Sheridan family believed their parents had fallen victim to an intruder, expecting the police to pursue this angle. However, within a week, the prosecutor's office issued statements to the public downplaying the risk of further incidents, suggesting confidence in the absence of an external threat. During a meeting with the brothers, Soriano and an assistant presented the theory of murder-suicide, citing hesitation wounds on John's body and announcing plans to investigate the couple's personal communications for any signs of issues that might support this theory.

The Sheridan sons were highly skeptical of the murder-suicide explanation, having observed no indications of problems between their parents that could lead to such a tragic outcome. Mark, familiar with the legal system, initially gave Soriano the benefit of the doubt but later expressed his doubts.

Mark later pointed out several indicators suggesting John had no intention of ending his life: purchasing new suits and shirts, engaging in a FaceTime call with a grandchild the evening before, and sending a detailed work-related email. Similarly, Joyce had been decorating the house for Halloween, a yearly tradition. Police records indicated only one emergency call from the Sheridan residence in their thirty-seven years of residence, related to a fall Joyce had suffered.

Upon receiving a suggestion from Somerset County prosecutor Geoffrey Soriano that a second, private autopsy might be beneficial due to the limited capabilities of the county medical examiner's office, the Sheridan family decided to engage the expertise of Michael Baden. Baden, a renowned former forensic pathologist with a notable tenure as the chief medical examiner for New York City and a host of HBO's "Autopsy," was brought in to collaborate with deputy state medical examiner Eddy Lilavois.

Baden and Lilavois concurred that the stab wounds on both John and Joyce Sheridan were inflicted by the same knife. However, they were unable to definitively determine if this knife was one of the two found at the scene. One of these knives, designed for slicing bread with its serrated blade and rounded tip, seemed an unlikely choice for inflicting such wounds. They speculated the possibility of a third, undiscovered knife being involved.

In their thorough investigation, detectives conducted interviews with 180 individuals, including friends, family, and co-workers of the Sheridans, but found no evidence of any significant personal issues that might have led to the tragedy. The only hint of potential distress came from John's professional sphere. Gary Lesneski, Cooper's chief counsel, mentioned John's concern over an anticipated state report on high fatality rates in the hospital's cardiac unit. However, John's communication, especially a detailed and composed email to George Norcross written the evening before the incident, displayed no signs of emotional turmoil.

The toxicology reports on John and Joyce Sheridan revealed no groundbreaking information. John's blood contained traces of his heart medication, while Joyce's system showed high levels of prescription painkillers, attributed to her long-term treatment following a back injury sustained in a fall during her last year as a schoolteacher in 1999.

DNA analysis conducted on the blood found on the knives yielded inconclusive results due to the limited sample size, only indicating that the blood originated from a white male.

Throughout the investigation, The Philadelphia Inquirer pursued legal action to gain access to the case reports and other related records. However, the court ruled in favor of the state, maintaining the confidentiality of these documents.

A notable development occurred around the time Mark Sheridan met with Prosecutor Geoffrey Soriano. The Sheridan brothers were granted permission to re-enter their family home after the crime scene investigation, which lasted about four hours, was completed. In the master bedroom, the epicenter of the fire, they stumbled upon a mysterious, melted metal object near where their father's body had been found.

The object, measuring 2 by 6.5 inches and weighing about 4.67 ounces, was primarily composed of zinc, with minor traces of aluminum and copper, as revealed by lab tests. Its original form was uncertain, leading to speculation among the brothers that it might have been the elusive third knife speculated in the case, though they also considered the possibility of it being a knob from the armoire.

Notably, forensic expert Henry Lee, a colleague of Michael Baden, expressed doubts about the object being a knife. He pointed out that zinc-based alloys are more typically used in cast metal products rather than knives, and its weight did not align with that of a typical knife.

Further complicating matters, if the object were indeed a knife, it didn't match the kitchen knife set from which the other two knives at the scene were sourced. These kitchen knives were made from chromium-iron alloys, which require much higher temperatures to melt than what would have been produced in the partial room fire at the Sheridan house. This was evidenced by the fact that John Sheridan's undershirt was only charred, not completely burned. Mark Sheridan expressed his frustration with these and other perceived oversights in the investigation in a detailed email to Prosecutor Soriano.

Another perplexing discovery was made a month after the fire. An insurance adjuster inspecting the house found a bent fireplace poker in a bathroom near the master bedroom, an unusual location given that the house had no upstairs fireplace. Although photographed on the day of the fire, it wasn't collected as evidence until the family requested it following the adjuster's discovery. The Sheridan brothers speculated that this poker might have been responsible for John Sheridan's broken ribs, rather than the armoire that had fallen on him.

The day after the discovery of the fireplace poker, Mark Sheridan confronted Lee Niles, a county investigator, in the front yard of the house. Mark recalled asking Niles about the conclusion of the case. Mark later recounted to The New York Observer that Niles denied having concluded it was a murder-suicide, a statement Mark viewed as dishonest, believing that the investigators had prematurely made up their minds.

In March 2015, Somerset County Prosecutor Geoffrey Soriano released a comprehensive report on the investigation into John Sheridan's death. The report, which marked a significant development in the case, concluded that there was no evidence of an intruder's presence in the Sheridan home at the time of the incident. Consequently, the death of John Sheridan, which had previously been categorized as undetermined, was reclassified as a suicide.

The report detailed the extensive investigative efforts undertaken, including 180 interviews and a thorough examination of the couple's records. Witnesses, albeit unnamed in the report, described John Sheridan as being excessively worried about an impending state report concerning issues in the cardiac unit where he worked. On the day of his death, John had reportedly planned a meeting with his hospital colleagues.

Robbery was dismissed as a motive for the crime. The investigators found that significant amounts of cash, jewelry, electronic devices, antiques, and prescription drugs of potential interest to a thief remained untouched in the house. There was also no evidence of forced entry into the Sheridan residence, and no reports of suspicious individuals in the area around the time of the fire. DNA analysis of the blood found on one of the knives at the scene was consistent with John Sheridan's.

Soriano's report, leaning on the absence of evidence supporting alternative theories, reaffirmed the initial hypothesis of a murder-suicide. The report did not delve into the specifics of the couple's final moments, whether their deaths were premeditated or the result of a spontaneous altercation. The presence of items like the gasoline can and kitchen knives suggested premeditation, but the report did not conclude on this aspect. John Sheridan's cause of death was attributed to a combination of a jugular vein wound and smoke inhalation.

In a rare interview regarding the report, Soriano addressed the mysterious melted object discovered by the Sheridan brothers. He expressed uncertainty about its nature, suggesting it could have been anything and emphasizing the focus on gathering all relevant evidence. When questioned about the lack of a convincing motive in the report, Soriano acknowledged the limitations, stating, "I don't know what else was going on in his life."

Mark Sheridan maintained regular communication with Prosecutor Geoffrey Soriano during the investigation into his parents' deaths and had the opportunity to review the report's final drafts before its release. However, Mark was in strong disagreement with the conclusions drawn in the report and publicly expressed his dissent. He emphasized that both he and his brothers lacked answers regarding the fate of their parents and believed that the investigation had not provided any definitive explanations either. In 2022, Mark criticized the investigation as inadequate and rushed, expressing frustration at the implications made about his father's actions and intelligence.

Mark contended that if his father had indeed intended to commit murder-suicide, he would have executed it in a way that left no room for doubt. He voiced his determination to protect his father's reputation from being tarnished by what he perceived as speculative conclusions based on an incomplete investigation.

The Sheridan family was not alone in their dissatisfaction with the official findings. John Sheridan's brother, Peter, a federal judge, lamented that the prosecutor's conclusions tarnished the legacy of John and Joyce Sheridan. Ed Stier, the first head of the state's Division of Criminal Justice, criticized the handling of the investigation, suggesting that the crime scene was compromised, making further forensic analysis difficult.

The Sheridan family's statement raised several questions, including the necessity of three knives in a murder-suicide scenario and the absence of Joyce's blood on John, despite her apparent struggle.

Forensic pathologist Michael Baden, in an affidavit for a court action filed by the Sheridan brothers, questioned the prosecutor's conclusions. He noted that John Sheridan showed no prior indications of suicidal thoughts or depression. Baden also doubted that any of the knives at the scene could have inflicted John's wounds, including the hesitation wounds. He also pointed out inconsistencies in the angle of John's neck wound and the lack of Joyce's blood on John's body.

Baden had forensic expert Henry Lee review the DNA results from the knives. While Soriano had indicated that the DNA matched John, the lab report only confirmed the DNA to be from a white male, not necessarily a Sheridan family member. Lee's analysis revealed a genetic pattern that did not match any male member of the Sheridan family.

Dennis Cogan, a former Philadelphia prosecutor turned defense attorney, reviewed Baden's affidavit and concurred with its skepticism. He suggested that the missing knife strongly indicated the involvement of a third person. Cogan criticized the investigative approach, arguing that the investigators seemed more intent on fitting the facts to their initial theory rather than objectively following the evidence.

According to Baden, the injuries sustained by John, including the broken ribs, could have been the result of multiple blows from the poker rather than the armoire falling on him. He also pointed out a chipped front tooth that was not initially documented in the autopsy report, a detail inconsistent with the expected bruising on the face if the armoire had caused it.

Barry Jansen, the police photographer, held a different perspective and did not see the presence of the poker as disproving the murder-suicide theory. He argued that if an intruder had used a fire poker to attack John, they would likely have continued the assault to ensure the job was finished. Jansen also questioned the intruder's motive for going downstairs to retrieve both the poker and the knives, finding the sequence of events nonsensical.

Barbara Boyer, a reporter for the Inquirer who had the opportunity to tour the house, found it entirely plausible that an intruder could have utilized the poker as a weapon of opportunity. She noted that the unlocked back door provided easy access to the poker located in close proximity to the fireplace and tool rack. Boyer considered the poker and knives as potential improvised weapons. A set of stairs from that area led to a second master bedroom door, which showed signs of possible disturbance during the incident.

Certain witnesses were not interviewed during the investigation, raising concerns about the thoroughness of the inquiry. Chris Stephens, a friend of Joyce's, had no recollection of Joyce ever expressing marital concerns or behaving unusually before her death. However, she was not contacted by the police for an interview. Mary Kay Roberts, a close associate of John for nearly twenty years, who had interacted with him shortly before the fire, also reported that she was not interviewed.

Additionally, a neighbor living near the Sheridan residence claimed that she was never interviewed by the police. She referred the reporter to another former neighbor, Tom Draper, who recounted an incident that occurred a week before the fire. Draper described encountering a parked vehicle in the cul-de-sac near his house early in the morning, which then hastily drove towards the Sheridan house before abruptly turning into a group of streets with no outlet, prompting his curiosity.

Forensic expert Baden expressed skepticism about the evidence pointing solely to an intruder, yet some signs hinted at such a possibility. Blood spatters on walls outside the bedroom and stairwell, which investigator Jansen was reportedly instructed not to record, seemed to align with an attack scenario, contradicting Soriano's claim that the violence was confined to the Sheridans' bedroom.

Soriano's analysis suggested these were transfer stains from firefighters during the body removal, yet Baden questioned this. The spatters, higher on the wall and distinct from the smeared stains, appeared more consistent with a stabbing. A retired Philadelphia detective and reporter Boyer, who toured the house with the Sheridans' permission, concurred.

The case took another turn with the question of fingerprints. The Sheridans criticized the investigation for dismissing an intruder theory without thoroughly checking for fingerprints or blood traces at the house's unlocked entries. Boyer discovered a bloody fingerprint inside the front door, and the scrutiny on whether the poker, found in a bathroom, was ever checked for prints intensified.

The case complexity deepened with Detective Jeffrey Scozzafava's whistle-blower lawsuit against the county. He accused officials of evidence mishandling in the Sheridan case and others, including lying about fingerprint searches outside the master bedroom. The detectives' claimed "flashlight technique" for finding prints was met with skepticism and disbelief by experts, including a former NYPD detective, and Scozzafava suggested this method was a fabrication.

Additionally, Scozzafava's lawsuit shed light on another potential fingerprint clue. Two months post-fire, John's driver's license surfaced at a college campus, miles away from Skillman. The student who found it, oblivious to John's demise, mailed it back. Although Scozzafava started fingerprint analysis on the license, his reassignment to another unit left the task incomplete.

The brothers Sheridan grappled with the improbability of the crime unfolding as the prosecutor envisioned. They privately contemplated whether their mother, known for her occasional angry outbursts, might have instigated a conflict that spiraled out of control. However, they realized the physical implausibility of this theory. Given Joyce's petite stature at 5-foot-2 and her chronic upper-back pain, it seemed unlikely she could have inflicted the fatal wound on John with the necessary force.

Mark Sheridan, while delving into his parents' financial affairs post-tragedy, stumbled upon a trove of documents. These papers suggested John Sheridan's concern over unethical dealings in certain land projects, including the L3 development in Camden. The documents hinted at possible foul play involving the Norcrosses, a powerful local family, in muscling out a favored developer. Mark shared these findings with legal authorities but received no concrete response.

Forensic pathologist Baden, analyzing the case, leaned towards the possibility of a double homicide. He found the murder-suicide theory unconvincing, particularly noting the atypical use of fire in such scenarios. Baden suggested reclassifying the case as "undetermined" due to insufficient evidence for a definitive homicide ruling.

Mark's dissatisfaction with the official narrative led him to resign as chief counsel for the New Jersey Republican Party, focusing on challenging the findings. Despite continuing to handle some cases for the party and Governor Christie, Mark felt a conflict of interest in his dual roles. He was determined to prevent Soriano's reappointment as prosecutor and offered a substantial reward for information leading to the resolution of his parents' mysterious deaths.

Mark Sheridan highlighted the broader issues plaguing New Jersey's medical examiner system while discussing his parents' case. He criticized the system as a disaster and stressed that medical examiners should operate independently, not as agents of the state or under law enforcement authority, a view echoed by former chief medical examiners of the state.

At the time of the Sheridans' deaths, New Jersey had not had a chief medical examiner for six years. Victor Weedn, who resigned in 2009, had expressed disappointment with the lack of oversight from the Attorney General and the state's Division of Criminal Justice. This vacancy was eventually filled by Andrew Falzon in June 2015, appointed by Governor Christie.

The inadequacies of the system were apparent at lower levels too. The Northern Regional Medical Examiner's office, which oversaw the work of Lilavois who performed the Sheridans' autopsies, had lost its reaccreditation. The state's toxicology lab also lacked proper accreditation, raising concerns about its testing credibility.

Lilavois, who conducted John Sheridan's autopsy, was not board certified in forensic pathology. His past included a controversial case in New York City, where he changed a child's cause of death from homicide to natural death without promptly informing relevant parties, leading to significant personal and investigative repercussions.

Mark Sheridan pointed out that due to the absence of a state medical examiner, there was no oversight of Lilavois' work on his father's autopsy, leading to inaccuracies in the report. Weedn and Faruk Presswala, another former chief medical examiner, noted that even with a chief medical examiner, oversight of county or regional examiners was limited, reducing the role to a figurehead.

Sheridan also criticized Lilavois's lack of independence from the prosecutor's office, suggesting that meetings with the prosecutor, Soriano, influenced the autopsy's conclusions. This concern was echoed by Lawrence Kobilinsky, chair of the science department at John Jay College of Criminal Justice, who argued for the necessity of independence between law enforcement and medical examiners. He advocated for medical examiners to fall under the jurisdiction of a state's health department to ensure impartiality and avoid biases inherent in law enforcement.

The Sheridans' public critique of Soriano and his report sparked some controversy. Notably, Raymond Bateman, a prominent figure in New Jersey politics and the Republican Party's gubernatorial candidate in 1977, penned an op-ed in the Middlesex County Home News Tribune to defend Soriano. Bateman had a personal connection to the case through his son Christopher, a State Senator who had backed Soriano's nomination.

In his op-ed, Bateman speculated that John Sheridan, whom he had known during his own tenure in the State Senate, might have been mentally unwell at the time of his death. He drew a parallel to Andreas Lubitz, the Germanwings Flight 9525 pilot who had crashed his plane due to severe depression. Bateman expressed a poignant perspective, suggesting that mental illness could profoundly alter a person's judgment.

While agreeing with the Sheridans about the shortcomings of New Jersey's medical examiner system, Victor Weedn, a former chief medical examiner, supported Lilavois' murder-suicide conclusion based on the autopsy reports. He observed that the couple's injuries generally aligned with this scenario, although he hadn't reviewed the photographic evidence. Weedn reasoned that an intruder or burglar typically confronts victims near an entry point on the ground floor, not in a bedroom. However, he acknowledged that homicide couldn't be entirely dismissed, especially if the weapon used in the attack remained unaccounted for.

In December 2014, Mark Sheridan and his brothers sought to have their father John's death classified as 'undetermined' by sending Baden's affidavit to state medical examiners. Despite no initial response, they warned the state of a potential lawsuit if John's death was officially ruled a suicide. Following the release of Soriano's report, they proceeded with their legal action.

The state's initial reaction was to seek dismissal of the lawsuit, claiming there was no legal basis to force a medical examiner to alter their opinion on the manner of death. However, a three-judge panel directed that the lawsuit should target the medical examiner's office.

In early 2016, as the lawsuit was underway, two key events lent support to the Sheridans' cause. Firstly, a public letter signed by over 200 notable New Jersey figures, including former governors and attorneys general, appealed for a revision of the death ruling. Secondly, Detective Jeffrey Scozzafava filed a whistleblower lawsuit, alleging serious mishandling of evidence in the

Sheridan case and retaliation against him for his complaints.

Scozzafava's lawsuit highlighted various procedural failings, such as inexperienced officers handling forensic evidence, improper storage and packaging of evidence, and a fabricated "flashlight technique" for fingerprint searching. He claimed these issues led to his reassignment to a less prestigious position, and he even witnessed crucial evidence being discarded.

In January 2017, a breakthrough came when State Medical Examiner Andrew Falzon revised John Sheridan's death to 'undetermined.' Despite believing the wounds were self-inflicted, Falzon noted the lack of a conclusive weapon and the fire-damaged scene as complicating factors. Mark Sheridan saw this as a partial vindication but acknowledged the journey ahead for full clarity.

The family urged for the case to be reopened and thoroughly reinvestigated. However, Mark expressed frustration five years later, noting that while the case was technically open, there seemed to be little active investigation, leaving them in a state of uncertainty.

Meanwhile, Scozzafava's lawsuit was dismissed, with the county arguing his motivations were trivial and he hadn't suffered any real harm. Scozzafava settled for $175,000 and signed a nondisclosure agreement, preventing further discussion about the alleged misconduct in the cases he had brought up.

As the Sheridan brothers' lawsuit was ongoing, Governor Chris Christie, once a federal prosecutor, chose not to reappoint Soriano for a second term in February 2016. Christie later explained his decision stemmed from a loss of confidence in Soriano. This decision was not only influenced by the Sheridan case but also by other cases where Soriano's office faced criticism. Michael Robertson, another former federal prosecutor who had worked under Christie, was appointed as Soriano's replacement.

Mark Sheridan welcomed this change, citing a history of failures in Soriano's office. However, State Senator Christopher Bateman, who had originally recommended Soriano, expressed disappointment. He suspected the decision's timing, closely following the public letter, indicated a connection to the Sheridan case and defended Soriano's handling of the investigation.

By the fall of that year, Soriano had taken a position as an assistant attorney general for the state.

In another development, two months after Christie's decision, Matt Sheridan, one of the Sheridan brothers, was indicted on a cocaine possession charge related to his arrest on the morning of his parents' deaths. Mark Sheridan criticized this move by the prosecutor's office as retaliatory, stemming from their efforts to amend their father's death certificate. He claimed this breached an assurance given by Soriano after the deaths. Due to the conflict between the family and the prosecutor's office, the Middlesex County prosecutor's office took over the case, although any trial would be held in Somerset County. Eventually, the charges against Matt were dropped following a ruling that the search leading to his arrest was illegal.

In early 2022, political consultant Sean Caddle admitted to orchestrating a murder in Hudson County. He had hired two men to kill Michael Galdieri, the son of a late state senator, in his Jersey City apartment in May 2014. The murder involved stabbing Galdieri and then setting a fire to hide the crime.

This case resonated with Mark Sheridan due to its striking resemblance to his parents' deaths, which also involved stabbings and a subsequent fire. In response, Mark wrote to the Somerset County prosecutor's office and Acting Attorney General Matt Platkin, pointing out the uncanny similarities and recalling how officials had previously dismissed the notion of a murder-for-hire scenario involving such methods.

Mark speculated on a possible connection between the two cases, particularly concerning a missing knife from his parents' home. He recalled how investigators had questioned him about a knife missing from their kitchen. Intriguingly, a "long-bladed butcher knife" was found in a pickup truck in Connecticut the day after his parents' deaths, belonging to George Bratsenis, a suspect in a bank robbery. Mark urged authorities to collaborate with Connecticut officials to examine this knife for any potential DNA link to his parents' case.

Bratsenis, a career criminal with ties to organized crime, was later identified as one of the hired killers in the Galdieri murder. The FBI took over the Galdieri case for undisclosed reasons. During Caddle's plea hearing, his lawyer mentioned Caddle's cooperation with the FBI on a significant investigation, hinting at broader implications. Under his plea agreement, Caddle faced a potential reduced sentence in exchange for his cooperation.

The sentencing was postponed until December, with many in New Jersey's political circles anticipating the case could escalate into a major corruption scandal. Despite no initial response to Mark's letters, Platkin's office announced the reopening of the Sheridan investigation at the end of May. The Sheridans had preserved sections of bloodstained drywall from their house as evidence before selling it. Mark remained skeptical about uncovering new evidence but was appreciative of the renewed investigation. The legal representatives for Bratsenis and Caddle did not comment on any contact with their clients, while Platkin stated that the investigation would follow the evidence wherever it led.

Murder of Missy Beavers

In the early hours of April 18, 2016, as the first light of dawn was yet to break, 45-year-old Terri "Missy" Bevers arrived at the Creekside Church of Christ in Midlothian, Texas. This was a routine for Bevers, a dedicated and passionate fitness instructor, known for her high-energy "gladiator boot camps" which had garnered a loyal and enthusiastic following. Her classes were not just workouts; they were events that her attendees eagerly anticipated.

That morning, however, marked a tragic deviation from her routine. Shortly after Bevers set foot in the church, a tragic fate awaited her. An assailant, lurking within the church premises and clad in police tactical gear from head to toe, brutally ended her life. This horrifying act took place in the quiet of the early morning, leaving the community in shock and disbelief.

Less than an hour later, when Bevers' body was discovered, her assailant had vanished into the darkness of the early morning, leaving behind a trail of unanswered questions and a community reeling from the loss of a beloved figure.

Terri "Missy" Bevers, born on August 9, 1970, in Graham, Texas, as reported by the Dallas Observer, had a life rich in personal and professional achievements. She was not just a fitness instructor; she was a teacher, a loving wife to Brandon Bevers since 1998, and a devoted mother to three daughters, aged 8, 13, and 15 at the time of her untimely death, as detailed by PEOPLE magazine.

Around 2014, Bevers realized a significant goal in her life - becoming a certified personal trainer. She joined Camp Gladiator, bringing her vibrant energy and unyielding commitment to fitness to the people of Midlothian. Her boot camps, usually held in the parking lot of the Creekside Church of Christ, were a mere twenty-minute drive from her home, a testament to her dedication to her local community.

However, on that ill-fated Monday, a severe thunderstorm in Midlothian prompted a change of plans. The 5 a.m. boot camp, instead of being held outdoors as usual, was moved inside the church. The inclement weather would have deterred a less committed instructor, but Bevers was unwavering in her dedication, determined to conduct her class regardless of the weather conditions.

The evening before the tragedy, Bevers had posted an enthusiastic and motivating message on Facebook: "NO EXCUSES... You are Gladiators!" This post, meant to inspire and rally her class, unknowingly played a role in the tragic events that followed. It inadvertently provided her killer with the precise location and time needed to carry out the heinous act.

On a stormy morning that would later be remembered for its tragic events, Terri "Missy" Bevers, driven by her unwavering dedication to her fitness class, arrived at the Creekside Church of Christ in Midlothian, Texas, at approximately 4:18 a.m. This detail, reported by CBS News, underscored Bevers' commitment to her profession and her students. In a practical move, she parked her vehicle near the church's front entrance, intending to efficiently unload her equipment for the morning's class.

However, unknown to Bevers, a sinister presence had already infiltrated the serene church grounds.

Earlier, at 3:50 a.m., the church's security system, activated by motion, had captured a chilling sight. An individual, shrouded in police tactical gear, had made their way into the church. The security footage showed this person meandering through the church hallways, their identity completely obscured by the comprehensive coverage of the gear, including a helmet. Notably, as reported by True Crime Edition, the individual had a distinctive walk, marked by an outward turn of their feet, particularly the right one, lending a peculiar aspect to their movements.

The church's security cameras also documented Bevers' arrival that morning but, tragically, failed to capture the horrendous act that would follow.

When Bevers' students arrived 45 minutes later, ready for their workout, they were met with a scene that would haunt them forever. They found their beloved instructor lifeless, her body bearing the brutal marks of puncture wounds to her head and chest.

The local police, unaccustomed to dealing with such heinous acts in their normally peaceful community, faced the daunting task of unraveling the mystery behind the murder of a wife and mother. At the crime scene, signs of forced entry into the church and into several rooms suggested a burglary attempt. However, as reported by WFAA, nothing appeared to have been stolen, leading investigators to speculate that the staged burglary was possibly a ruse to mask the killer's true motive.

A key piece of evidence emerged from the height analysis of the suspect captured in the video. Estimates placed the suspect's height between 5 feet 2 inches and 5 feet 8 inches. Furthermore, the suspect's unique gait opened up the possibility that the assailant might not necessarily be a male. Police appealed to the public for any information that could aid their investigation.

The inquiry naturally extended to those closest to Bevers, including her husband, Brandon Bevers. He was initially a person of interest until his alibi, a fishing trip in Mississippi, was verified. Brandon expressed his inability to comprehend who would want to harm, much less murder, his wife.

The investigation took a turn when a search warrant for Bevers' cellphone records, spanning from March 1 to April 24, unveiled a tumultuous side to her personal life. There was evidence of "an ongoing financial and marital struggle as well as intimate/personal relationships external to the marriage." Text messages suggested extramarital affairs, adding complexity to the case.

Intriguingly, police discovered that Bevers had been receiving intimate and flirtatious messages over LinkedIn. Some of these messages had been deleted and were reportedly irretrievable. This discovery led to a crucial revelation: Bevers had shown a friend a private LinkedIn message from an unidentified man, received just three days before her murder. Both Bevers and her friend had found the message unsettling, describing it as "creepy and strange."

Despite these revelations and the seemingly imminent danger, Bevers appeared unsuspecting on the morning of her death, leaving her licensed firearm in her car, a decision that underscored the unexpected and brutal nature of the attack that claimed her life.

As the investigation intensified, a new figure of interest emerged, drawing the attention of both the police and the public. This individual was none other than Randy Bevers, Missy's father-in-law. His involvement in the case began under suspicious circumstances that raised many eyebrows.

On April 22, merely four days after the tragic incident, Randy Bevers visited a local dry cleaner with an item that would soon become a significant point of inquiry — a woman's shirt soaked in blood. To the employee at the dry cleaner, he provided a seemingly innocuous explanation: the blood was from a dog. Randy recounted an incident where he had intervened in a dog fight and, in the process, had carried an injured, bleeding dog to a veterinarian.

However, the employee, sensing something amiss, alerted the police. This action propelled Randy Bevers into the spotlight as a potential suspect. Notably, his physical build was somewhat similar to that of the person seen in the church's security footage, and he walked with a noticeable limp, further piquing the investigators' interest.

The police delved into verifying his alibi. It turned out that Randy had been in California with his wife at the time of the murder, a fact that was confirmed and supported by his daughter's testimony regarding the dog fight. Further investigation, including a forensic analysis of the blood-stained shirt, corroborated Randy's story — the blood was indeed from a dog, leading the police to exclude him from their list of suspects.

In the following weeks, the investigation took another turn when a new piece of evidence surfaced. Hours before Missy Bevers was murdered, a suspicious vehicle was captured by security cameras circling the parking lot of a sporting goods store near the church. The car, described in police reports as possibly a 2010–2012 Nissan Altima or a similar model, lingered in the parking lot for an unusual length of time, often with its lights turned off. This behavior was deemed suspicious enough to warrant public attention.

The police released the footage, appealing to the community for information regarding the vehicle and its owner. Despite this effort, the mystery surrounding the car deepened as its owner remained unidentified.

In a continued effort to unravel the identity of the suspect, the FBI enlisted the expertise of a forensic podiatrist to analyze the security footage. The focus was on the suspect's peculiar gait, which had been a point of interest from the beginning. However, as reported by CBS News, the podiatrist concluded that the suspect's unusual walk was likely a result of the weight of their gear, leaving the investigators without a definitive lead on the suspect's gender.

It was in late 2019, three years after the tragic incident, that detectives decided to revisit a tip that had repeatedly surfaced during the course of their investigation. This tip centered around a former tactical police officer named Bobby Wayne Henry.

Henry emerged as a person of significant interest for several reasons. Firstly, he had openly admitted to possessing his riot gear, although he claimed that it no longer fit him. This detail was particularly intriguing given the suspect's attire seen in the church's security footage. Secondly, Henry was known to attend mass at the very church where Bevers was murdered, the Creekside Church of Christ. Adding to the growing suspicion was his physical impairment; he walked with a noticeable limp, mirroring the unique gait of the suspect captured on video.

Another critical aspect that drew the investigators' attention was his vehicle. Henry owned a car that bore a striking resemblance to a different vehicle of interest in the case — a dark SUV that was reported to have been seen leaving the church on the morning of Bevers' murder.

With these coincidences piling up, Henry seemed to be a promising lead. However, a significant discrepancy soon arose. Henry stood at 6 feet 1 inch tall, a stature that was inconsistent with the height estimates of the suspect seen in the security footage. Additionally, as the investigation delved deeper, Henry's alibi for the time of the murder was thoroughly verified and ultimately corroborated. Consequently, he was ruled out as a person of interest in the case.

Fast forward to 2021, five years since the untimely death of Missy Bevers, the Midlothian Police Department made a significant announcement. As reported by Fox News, a retired federal law enforcement agent had joined the team of investigators working on Bevers' case. This development indicated that the authorities were still actively pursuing leads and were committed to solving the case. The police department assured the public and Bevers' family that the case was far from being considered cold, signaling their unwavering determination to bring closure to this perplexing and heart-wrenching mystery.

Bibliography

Sruthi, V. "Who Killed Rev Paul Jones? Who Is Rev Paul Jones? What Was Rev Paul Joness Cause Of Death?", FreshersLive, 6 Feb. 2023, https://www.freshe rslive.com/latest/articles/who-killed-rev-paul-jones-who-is-rev-paul-jon es-what-was-rev-paul-joness-cause-of-death-10005317

B, Debbie "Melody Ann Jones: Murder victim or Cold-blooded killer?", True Crime Diva, 15 July 2019, https://truecrimediva.com/melody-ann-jones/

Bullard, Stephan; et al. (2012). The Silver Bridge Disaster of 1967. Charleston, S.C.: Arcadia Publishing.

B, Debbie, "Who killed Jennifer Lockmiller?", True Crime Diva, 12 Oct 2019, https://truecrimediva.com/jennifer-lockmiller/

Kane, Karla, "Longtime journalist's book takes a deep dive into an infamous Peninsula murder", Pleasanton Weekly, Sep 18, 2023, https://www.pleasanto nweekly.com/news/2023/09/18/longtime-journalists-book-takes-a-deep-dive-into-an-infamous-peninsula-murder

Whelan, Michael, "Arlis Perry", Unresolved, March 24, 2016, https://unres olved.me/arlis-perry

B, Debbie, "Deadly Explosion Killed God-Fearing Couple in 1982", True Crime Diva, Jne 19, 2020, https://truecrimediva.com/deadly-explosion-kille d-god-fearing-couple-in-1982/

Whiticker, Alan (2006). Searching for the Beaumont Children: Australia's Most Famous Unsolved Mystery. John Wiley & Sons Australia.

Whelan, Michael, "The Beaumont Children", Unresolved, n.d., https://unre solved.me/the-beaumont-children

B, Debbie, "Who Murdered Colorado College Student Denise Davenport?", True Crime Diva, July 2 2023, https://truecrimediva.com/denise-davenport/

Worrell, Georgia, "Cold case: 37 years this week since Denise Davenport

was found dead", Longmont Leader, April 14, 2022, https://www.longmontle
ader.com/crime/cold-case-37-years-this-week-since-denise-davenport-w
as-found-dead-5263995

Shugerman, Emily, "Tamla Horsford Died at a Slumber Party in 2018. Her
Family Still Wants Answers.", The Daily Beast, June 21 2020, https://www.the
dailybeast.com/tamla-horsford-died-at-a-slumber-party-in-2018-her-fa
mily-still-wants-answers

Pasqualini, Kym, "Morgan Violi: Decades-Old Murder Case Haunts a
Kentucky Community", The Crime Wire, Dec 26 2023, https://thecrimew
ire.com/true-crime/morgan-violi-decades-old-murder-case-haunts-a-ke
ntucky-community

Soliz, Steve, "Unsolved Northwest: Who Killed Misty Copsey?", King 5, Nov
9 2023, https://www.king5.com/article/news/crime/unsolved/misty-copsey-
disappearance-remained-unsolved-for-decades/281-071fadd1-538a-43d1-
8282-401c3c0d4119

Wikipedia contributors. "Murder of Adrian Donohoe." Wikipedia, The
Free Encyclopedia. Wikipedia, The Free Encyclopedia, December 21, 2023.
https://en.wikipedia.org/wiki/Murder_of_Adrian_Donohoe.

Sokolove, Michael, "Who killed the Sheridans?", New York Times, Feb. 5,
2016, https://www.nytimes.com/2016/02/07/magazine/who-killed-the-she
ridans.html

Truesdell, Jeff, "Mother-in-Law of Texas Fitness Instructor Killed in
Church Shares Family's Frustration a Month After Murder: 'When They Make
an Arrest, Will We Feel Like Celebrating?", People, May 27, 2016, https://peo
ple.com/crime/missy-bevers-murder-mother-in-law-asks-will-we-feel-li
ke-celebrating-arrest/